STEWART COPELAND
DRUMMING IN THE POLICE AND BEYOND
BY JOE BERGAMINI

Produced by Rob Wallis

Cover and book design by Michael Hoff
Cover photo (upper left) courtesy of Dietmar Clös
Cover photo (lower right) back cover photo by Danny Quatrochi

Fact-checking and additional editing: Dietmar Clös and Jeff Seitz
Copyediting: Greg Burrows

Music engraving: Brad Schlueter
Transcriptions: Joe Bergamini, Mike Sorrentino, Christian Johnson

Photographs courtesy of Dietmar Clös, Craig Betts, Danny
Quatrochi, Lissa Wales, Paul Natkin, Jeff Seitz, Robert Downs, Joe
Bergamini and Jim Pettit
Additional photos courtesy of Hoshino (U.S.A.)/Tama Drums (Jim
Gallagher)

Chronology and photo assistance by Dietmar Clös of The
PoliceWiki: thepolicewiki.org

Synchronicity percussion riser diagram by Joe Gorelick

November 29, 1979; The Palladium, New York (Photo courtesy Dietmar Clös).

CONTENTS

FOREWORD

STEW-DADDY-O

It's a blessing and curse at the same time: the wonderful yet often painful, double-edged sword that is known as dating one of the hottest girls in high school. My girlfriend looked very much like Marie Osmond, and in those days, Marie was the lustful focus of many an adolescent male fantasy. Plus, coupled with her Pat Benatar haircut, my high school girlfriend was a heartbreaker—and she knew it. Though the moments alone together were full of squishy, passionate bliss, the times in public often led to hard stares from muscle-bound, testosterone-laden young bucks who tended to look at me, then at her and project, without saying a single word, but with dagger-like eyes, "What the hell are you doing with *this* guy?!" It was enough to chisel at the self-confidence of any young lad, and no matter how fancifully I could waggle my fingers on my electric bass guitar, the experience made me an insecure, jealous wreck. So, when said girlfriend announced her absolute love for the band The Police, and especially her crush on the wiry blonde drummer named Stewart, I immediately hated him.

For her birthday I broke down and bought the recently released *Ghost in the Machine* on cassette and, on the way home from the record store, I decided to pop the tape into the Pioneer stereo in my gold 1968 Mercury Cougar. On came "Spirits in the Material World." The first thing I noticed about the music was the "in yer face" hi-hat. Then came that signature Stewart Copeland "crack" from the snare, the likes of which I had just never heard anywhere else before, and, to top it all off, *it came in backwards!* (At least from my young perspective.) At that time in my life, I was a Rush aficionado and anything lesser in complexity paled in my mind. Although these Police songs were short pop tunes filled with Sting's hypnotic, repetitive bass parts and Andy's glorious, textural guitarscapes, I was mainly sucked in by the intricacies of the hi-hat and ride cymbal work that layered over the solid backbone of the snare and punching kick drum. But what really sunk the hook in was the surprise and uniqueness of where this mad drummer would emphasize the bar, often placing the kick on the "ands" between the beats and emphasizing the "3."

"Who the hell does that?" I thought as I cruised the Cougar through the streets of Berkeley.

As part of my girlfriend's birthday present, I had picked up a pair of Police tickets for an upcoming show at the Cow Palace in San Francisco. She was overjoyed to be able to see the infamous "Three Blonde Heads" that adorned the walls of her bedroom in person and though the seats weren't great (we literally sat behind the stage), it gave me a bird's eye view of the raw energy and sweaty magnificence of Mr. Stewart Copeland. There he was, bashing away with the energy of a pissed-off ape, almost pushing the sticks through the drums. The whole drum riser shook and trembled with each hit as he stomped into the kick drum. Yet there was a grace to all this as well; he had method and precision to his bash as he drove the band like a horny stallion, daring them and the audience to hang on for this manic ride. I was blown away, as apparently was my girlfriend who squealed and squirmed with every beat. I remember vividly how a young woman was holding a white cardboard sign near the ramp where the band exited the stage. On the sign were scrawled the words "FUCK ME STEWART." The road crew got a kick out of it and made a point to illuminate her and the sign with their flashlights as Stewart ran down the ramp with a towel over his head. Upon seeing this, my girlfriend gave me a sheepish, somewhat guilty look.

From that point on, I absorbed everything Copeland, from The Police to *The Rhythmatist*, to his guest spots on not only a Peter Gabriel recording, but also an episode of the cult Brit comedy *The Young Ones*. But it was his work on Francis Ford Coppola's *Rumble Fish* where I finally recognized his true musical flare and signature. The textures and tones not sounding like anything that had come down the pike prior, it was a mesmerizing soundscape that to this day stands on its own.

I went on to form Primus in 1984 and though we had numerous drummers before landing on the mighty Tim "Herb" Alexander, it was always our intention to try to get that elusive Stewart Copeland snare and hi-hat sound whenever we entered the studio to record. We tried all types of snare and hi-hat sizes, different heads, different tunings. I'd like to think we came close, but I doubt it. Jump forward to 1998 when it was suggested to us that Primus work with a producer. We opted to not work with one person, but a series of musicians whom we found inspirational. Stewart's name was on the short list and when he surprisingly agreed to participate, we suggested an impromptu jam at a rehearsal spot in Los Angeles. We arrived before he did, but his drums were already set up and ready; the heads were dinged and dented, the cymbals tarnished, not at all what we expected. We each took turns sitting on the kit and tapping away. It sounded like a regular old kit, nothing special or different to give it that sound we'd always pursued. In came Stewart, with his off-white cardigan sweater tied around his neck like he had just come from watching Buffy and Midge play tennis at the local polo club. His demeanor was bright and friendly; that familiar deep, yet eager voice bouncing through the air. We were all in awe. After the normal familiarities, we took position to have a quick jam. Brain (Brian Mantia) was the Primus drummer at that time, and he jumped on his kit next to Stewart. I'm not sure who started what, but soon we were jamming along on nothing in particular, and I remember thinking, "There it is, that Stewart Copeland drum sound." I would look to Stewart as we were playing. He had this expression on his face that I've since experienced many times. It's an expression only Stewart has, sort of an intense stare of probing concentration mixed with the look of a deer in the headlights. On that day, it scared the shit out of me, and I could only look into his eyes briefly before having to turn away or look at the floor.

Stewart went on to produce a tune on the Primus *Antipop* record. We became friends and remained in contact. It wasn't until I asked Trey Anastasio if he'd like to participate in a jam-oriented show in New Orleans in 2000 that the notion of a Stewart collaboration came up. Trey expressed how much he'd always wanted to do a project with myself and Stewart Copeland and if I could get him involved, he'd be happy to do the show. (It wasn't until years later that I found out Trey was actually trying to get out of doing the gig, assuming there was no way that I could land Stewart.)

"I've been waiting for this phone call for twenty-five years!" was the response that bellowed through the phone when I

presented the notion to Stewart. Oysterhead was born.

I've since become quite familiar with Stewart and his drumming, and like being behind the scenes at Disneyland, I've become privy to some of his magic tricks. I don't know how often I've started a groove only to have Stewart come in backwards. I've realized that it's only backwards to me (and quite possibly the rest of the world), but Stewart knows exactly where he is and exactly what he's doing. I've always been intrigued by people who look at the world just a bit differently than the rest of us. Perhaps they see the color blue, or a tree, or a piece of cardboard differently than the average Joe. Stewart does that with rhythm and time. As a youth I was always perplexed and intrigued by this. In the song "One World (Not Three)," containing one of my favorite Police beats, Stewart anticipates the snare drop on the first backbeat, and it is mind-blowing how it propels the song forward and expands the dynamic. He does similar things often in his work. When I've asked him about this, Stewart generally replies that Western

music was secondary to him, having grown up in Middle East, and that Arabic music, his first sonic exposure, tends to emphasize the "3" in the bar. I've also come to learn that he is quite dyslexic, often writing down phone numbers backwards. As much as he may not want to admit it, I think this is also a clue to what gives Stewart such an amazing and unique rhythmic thumbprint. How different would Django Reinhardt's music sound if his hand had not been altered by an injury? Stewart is a direct reflection of his surroundings, experiences and unique perspective. He is one of the most honest drummers I've ever come across. The eclectic and often abstract nature of his creations flow from him seldom impeded. I'm amused by this because when Oysterhead first started recording, Stewart, being from one of the most successful mainstream groups ever, would tout his "pop sensibilities" as this grand asset to the group. But as we moved through the project, I came to find that the most abstract material was the stuff he naturally gravitated towards or even created ("Wield the Spade"!).

As far as his tonality, I'm often reminded of the first time he, Trey and I got together for a jam in Vermont. It was in The Barn, a studio Trey had built out of 200-year-old timbers on his property. The only drum set available was this vintage Ludwig kit with thick, ancient, brown-stained heads on it. The snare was something that looked like it came from someone's tweaker uncle's closet and the cymbals appeared as if they were from the '60s and had spent the last few decades stored in a damp root cellar. It was a dark, dank drum set that even a drunken bar band would thumb their noses at. Stewart set up and started playing. Lo and behold, it sounded exactly like the Stewart Copeland I'd studied all those years: cracking snare, crispy

hi-hat and all. That experience reinforced a story that a friend of mine once regaled to me. He had met his hero, Robin Trower and was querying him on how he got his massive, unique tone. Robin answered in a thick British accent, "It's in me fingers, lad!" That's how it is with Stewart. I've seen him play on many drum kits of various sizes, shapes and timbres. It always sounds like Stewart Copeland. It's more about how he attacks his instrument than the instrument itself.

I've known Stewart for over twenty years now and I can proudly say that he is one of my best friends. He is an extremely intelligent, fascinating and wonderfully quirky individual. The conversations we have are always stimulating, often hilarious and I rarely can go more than a few weeks without a good Stew-daddy conversational fix via phone. It's amazing to meet one of your heroes and not only collaborate with them but have them become a big part of your life and you a part of theirs. He is my brother in so many ways and it is an honor to write up this foreword.

In conclusion, I'd wager that many of us male musicians were introduced to the music of The Police via our girlfriend's obsessions with "The Three Blonde Heads," but I'd further wager that most of us stuck around because of Stewart Copeland's playing. It is a very rare occasion when a band can succeed on that level of pop superstardom and still have such unique virtuosity. Where I grew up, when it concerned The Police, the girls went to see Sting, and the musicians went to see Stewart—except maybe my high school girlfriend and that woman at the Cow Palace with the "FUCK ME STEWART" sign.

Les Claypool

January 20,1980, Clark's Gym, State University of New York at Buffalo: My first concert as a crew member with The Police. The drums were set up, the band charged on to the stage and as drummer Stewart Copeland, whose name I had only learned a week or so earlier, pounded out the drum intro to "Next to You", my first thought was, "Why is this guy beating the crap out of the drums? Is he really angry?" And then as the song progressed and the intensity continued my second thought was, "Oh, I get it, he must have been a jock (athlete) who learned to play drums in college and got a gig with this new English punk band!"

I had come from a different world, drumming-wise. I had studied percussion at The Juilliard School, had lessons with notable drum set instructors, and strived to perfect the techniques of the many fusion and progressive drummers of the period. I wasn't unfamiliar with New Wave music but the energy of punk was something that had bypassed me entirely. And that punk energy is what was seemingly powering Stewart's performance, or so I thought.

After several concerts on what was a two-week close-out U.S. tour for the album *Reggatta de Blanc*, I began to sense something unique was happening. The punk energy I mentioned wasn't what was driving Stewart. It was his own personal and creative energy pouring out in all directions. A new and unique drumming style was being born as well as a drum sound that was completely his own, a drum sound that I began to embrace and hoped to maintain and enhance. Stewart was indeed "pushing the envelope" in the world of drumming. For myself, I began to realize that the energy Stewart was projecting was something that had been waning over the years in my own playing, and I was glad to rediscover it.

Due to several years of intense studio work, post-Police touring years, I had forgotten what it was like to experience Stewart's drumming in a live band situation again. He had been asked to assemble a band for the purpose of performing at a charity event. While sitting near him in a small rehearsal studio I was reminded of the power and energy that was so key to Stewart's playing style. With the many projects we have worked on together, those performance observations have repeated over the years.

Working with Stewart on records, scoring visual media, and live concerts over the years has been a journey of musical and visual discovery. His wisdom, insights, and intelligence are boundless. His drumming interests have branched out into a multitude of arenas. As a composer, his interest and love of all types of musical genres has energized his curiosity, and he continues to experiment with all types of compositional opportunities. Operas, concertos, ballet, theater, and world music, to name a few, are all in his sphere of interest, as well as diving into that good old rock 'n' roll spirit.

Our friendship and family ties have been interlocked for many years and I cherish the relationship. I look forward to many more years of being involved directly or indirectly in whatever Maestro Copeland sets his hand to.

Jeff Seitz

INTRODUCTION

Certain memories cement themselves with sight, sound and smell, and stay with you. I can close my eyes and be a teenager again in the Livingston Mall, circa 1982. I can smell the French fries and see the arcade game screens, and I can hear "Spirits in the Material World" and "Every Little Thing She Does is Magic" playing loudly in the record store there as I looked for the latest cool music. Those songs were everywhere, and that summer down at the Jersey Shore, dozens of kids were walking around in *Ghost in the Machine* T-shirts. I thought it was Japanese writing on the front. The Police were *everywhere*. The rhythms in those songs intrigued me; I had never heard grooves like them before, and the songs were so catchy that they stuck in my head. The following year, I kept seeing the video for "Wrapped Around Your Finger" on MTV. I would run a tape in our family's new VCR when a video came on that showed my favorite drummers—there were no drum videos or YouTube, of course—to capture a few seconds where I could check out the drum setup. The drumming on the song was unstoppably creative, and as the camera panned around the kit, with its cool-looking octobans sticking out to one side and various splash cymbals and bells adorning the front, I knew I had found another drummer who would be put under my personal microscope.

Of course, I was not the only one. Stewart Copeland was inducted to the *Modern Drummer* Hall of Fame in 2005, joining an elite list of the drummers who have been trendsetters in the playing of the drum set. There are leading rock drummers like Taylor Hawkins and Travis Barker who openly state they were influenced by Copeland, but really, drummers across all ages and styles list him as an inspiration. I think it's fair to say that he changed the game for every rock drummer who came after him. His approach, which is the topic of this book, is truly a unique voice on the instrument. If the highest goal in drumming is to serve the music while creating an instantly identifiable sound and vocabulary, Stewart Copeland is without a doubt in the pantheon of greats.

For this book, I sought to provide insight into Copeland's development as a drummer, and then delve deeply into his work with The Police. Stories about the relationships among Sting, Stewart, and Andy Summers are not the focus here; I was able to discuss some of this with him, but it is only included in these pages where it provides insight into how he approached his work. As you begin to study the transcriptions contained in this book, you will quickly learn that Stewart did not just develop a strong personal voice on the drums, he also used the recording studio as a tool or medium to create the parts he thought fit the songs. This included overdubbing parts wherever it felt right, and using effects, especially delay, to create a part for the song. He saw these things as simply part of the creative process. We have tried to document them carefully here, striking a balance between clarity and accuracy to the note. For instance, in "Walking on the Moon," Stewart wanted us to document every delayed note, since he played off those delayed notes to create his part; it was in essence part of the song. This makes the transcription very dense, but it is intriguing to study. For each song, where necessary, we provide notes about how we handled documenting the delay: in some songs we use only text in the manuscript to show it, while in other charts there is notation representing delayed notes. For some of his solo and soundtrack work ("Too Kool to Kalypso," "Koteja (Oh Bolilla)," "Don't Box Me In"), the parts are so layered that we use a grand staff to document them. In these cases, an additional key is provided.

The most exciting part of writing this book was a series of Zoom interviews that Rob Wallis and I were able to conduct with Stewart. He spent hours with us, answering all our questions and regaling us with stories of the old days—and the current days! We truly want to thank him for being so open with us—and *really fun* to talk with. While he has told (and extensively written about) stories of The Police many times, he indulged my drummers' deep dive into the minutiae of his drumming: coming up with parts, how he learned the songs, which snare drum he used, how his setup developed, which heads and cymbals were used, where he was set up in the studio, how many takes were done, and so on. For these questions, we feel we have assembled an unequaled document of his work. Where Stewart could not remember a detail, he directed me to people who could, especially his longtime drum tech Jeff Seitz and PoliceWiki co-founder/Police historian Dietmar Clös. Both gentlemen have been indispensable in getting the facts straight here, and I thank them profusely.

As I have done in all my transcription books, I have strived here for note-for-note accuracy. As the work progressed, I realized that in order to complete this in a timely fashion, I might need help, and I loved the idea of getting a couple of colleagues who love Stewart's playing to share in the project. I thank my old friend Mike Sorrentino and newer friend Christian Johnson for their detailed work on the charts, and Brad Schlueter for his masterful engraving. We think you'll find some truly inspiring listening as you sit with, study, and play the songs.

As with my previous work *Neil Peart: Taking Center Stage*, this book is much more than just a drum transcription book. In addition to the text documenting Stewart's career and work, plus the many transcriptions, we have presented many never-before-seen photos from throughout Stewart's career and organized them to match the era and album. There are also lots of old magazine ads and drum catalog images that will satisfy you if you are a drum gear geek like me.

Copeland's drumming with The Police is the stuff of legend, but he is a prolific composer who has amassed a huge body of work outside of the band. While his numerous film scores are outside the scope of this book, we have included a look at much of his other drum set work outside The Police, including his early project Klark Kent; *The Rhythmatist*, his album documenting his travels to Africa; his first film soundtrack, *Rumble Fish*; and his playing in post-Police bands Animal Logic, Oysterhead and Gizmodrome, each of which have a different musical environment to which he adapts while retaining his unique voice.

Most drummers who have casually listened to Stewart know that he was the first mainstream rock drummer to incorporate reggae concepts as a core of his playing, but there is *a lot* more to him than that. As you dig deeper into the layers of his work, you will discover that he has a very deep well of intention and concept in all aspects of his playing, which includes the choice of notes played, phrasing, density, composition, and also the tuning, effects, sound and overall percussive environment including overdubs and other instruments. Whether you want to dissect every delayed note of "Walking on the Moon," or just want to enjoy an overview of the storied career of one of the true rock greats, I think you'll find your trip into Stewart Copeland's world as fun and inspiring as I have.

Joe Bergamini, August 2021

ABOUT THE TRANSCRIPTIONS

When Joe asked me if I'd be interested in transcribing some of Stewart's playing on a few songs by The Police, I jumped at the chance. Stewart's drumming, and pretty much everything else about that band, had a giant influence on my early development on our instrument. Coming back to it after all these years with a very different perspective was equal parts enlightening, frustrating, challenging, and last but not least, fun. As I dug into some of these songs that I'd heard for so many years, my inner drum nerd was in full glory. The process was filled with several aha moments, from figuring out the overdubbed parts, to developing a system to notate delays, and more. Much of Stewart's drumming greatness comes from his vibe—and that cannot be notated. I've done the best I can to write what I hear, and I'm sure some of it can be subject to interpretation. I hope we're able to give you a little help in gaining a deeper insight into Stewart's work. Have fun.

Mike Sorrentino

Working on this book taught me that I can break the rules. I came into this project expecting to transcribe drum set parts—kick, snare, hi-hat, drum fills—but I couldn't have been more wrong. Stewart's approach is the definition of creating *rhythms that serve the music*. Stewart didn't limit himself to being a drum set player and he didn't just come up with drum set parts. Instead, he broke every single unwritten rule about being a drummer, and it's changed the way I think of my own playing. For example, I typically limit myself to four-limb independence behind the kit because I've always believed that's how it's done. Well, Stewart doesn't really follow that rule. If he's playing hi-hat and wants a ride bell to pop in for a few measures, he'll just dub it in. Or maybe he'll program the kick and snare electronically and play octoban fi s all drenched in delays or effects that made it difficult to figure out what he was playing, but to Stewart, it's never been about creating a perfectly clear drum recording for us drummers. It's obvious that the only rule he follows is to make good music. It was fascinating to break down these songs, because Stewart made these sorts of musical decisions in all of his projects. On top of all this were also the moments when Stewart did just play the full kit. It was magic in the making. He's absolutely capable of hanging with the best

drum set players of all time, and those moments made the project all the more fun. Not only has working on this project been eye-opening, I noticed that it took some of my own self-imposed stress out of the writing process. It was like having permission from one of the greats to trash my old rule book and play the parts I heard rather than the parts I could play with just my two hands and feet.

Christian Johnson

Stewart Copeland has always been a huge influence on my drumming. Transcribing and notating the music in this book has reminded me of how deeply an impression his playing has made on me, as well as countless other drummers. It seems impossible to have heard his drumming with The Police and not have been inspired by it. His groundbreaking style on the drums helped popularize reggae, requiring every drummer to learn a bit of the style, while attracting countless new fans to the genre. How many drummers would even think of owning a splash cymbal if it weren't for Stewart Copeland? Prior to him, splash cymbals weren't commonly used beyond jazz and Dixieland music, and certainly not in rock.

But it is his drumming that continues to inspire. His playing is never just supportive, but always propels the music forward in interesting and creative ways. He's an exciting player to listen to, partly because he is always exploring and "going for it." I learned a few things in the process of engraving the music in this book. Even though I'd seen The Police, I never realized was that he used delay units live in concert, improvising with them. I'd mistakenly assumed that was something only done in the studio during the mixing process. While I was aware that he'd overdubbed parts on "Every Breath You Take," I was unaware that he did that in other songs as well, as a means of creating interesting textures and composing the layered parts found on many of his recordings.

This book has been a pleasure to work on, both because I have rediscovered so much of Stewart's great drumming, but also for the opportunity to work with the great team behind it.

Brad Schlueter

NOTATION KEY

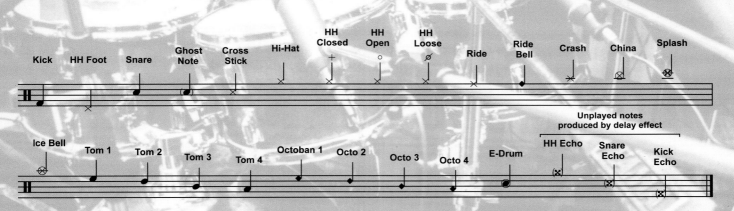

Kick · HH Foot · Snare · Ghost Note · Cross Stick · Hi-Hat · HH Closed · HH Open · HH Loose · Ride · Ride Bell · Crash · China · Splash

Unplayed notes produced by delay effect

Ice Bell · Tom 1 · Tom 2 · Tom 3 · Tom 4 · Octoban 1 · Octo 2 · Octo 3 · Octo 4 · E-Drum · HH Echo · Snare Echo · Kick Echo

PART 1

INFLUENCES
EARLY DRUMMING
& EARLY CAREER

Miles & Stewart Copeland (Photo by Lissa Wales).

ARABIC RHYTHMS

Though born in America, Stewart left the United States as a two-month-old baby and didn't return for 18 years. His family moved to Cairo, Egypt soon after his birth, and then to Beirut, Lebanon when he was five. Thus, he grew up immersed in Arabic culture, history, and music. The indigenous rhythms of the Middle East were heard and absorbed on a subconscious level by Stewart. "The drummers mostly played on little darbuka drums, and the rhythms they played were the overall rhythm of the music," he recalls. "The baladi rhythm and the dabki dance had a very distinctive rhythm, in which the emphasis was on the third beat of the bar, and they hid beat one, which is very similar to the mechanics of reggae. There's a buoyancy that comes from the interaction between the downbeat and upbeat that makes any music work," he continues. "The perfect Golden Square of rhythm is the balance between the kick and the backbeat. It's so perfect; that's why it has lasted over a hundred years. Reggae and the baladi are two other beats that aren't nearly as pan-global, but they are also very effective fundamental formulae for music."

The term "baladi" is used to describe several different rhythmic forms in Arabic music, and living in Cairo and Beirut, Stewart was constantly hearing these different rhythms. Many of these rhythms accompanied dances, so they had a strong pulse, but not the same pulse as the Western backbeat feeling. The ayoub rhythm is very common the Middle East, and it has a pulse resembling reggaeton. The baladi has several forms, sometimes emphasizing the "and" of beat one (with a long tone, or "doum" on the one), and sometimes emphasizing the

Stewart Copeland, Cairo, Egypt (Photo courtesy Stewart Copeland).

"and" of beat two (with long tones on the downbeat and upbeat of one). Both of these forms also add an accent on beat four. Stewart does not recall memorizing the grooves consciously, but the drive and flow of these rhythms is clearly present in his drumming.

While the American/rock influence (discussed below) was important, the "Arabic cultural DNA" Stewart acquired living in Beirut and Cairo left an indelible rhythmic consciousness that he drew upon as he learned to play the drums. "It's only as an adult," Stewart says, "that I look back on that Arabic culture that surrounded me and appreciate the value of it. It gave me a head start in reggae, for one thing!" While these Arabic influences may have crept in just through absorption, Stewart didn't specifically try to integrate any of it into his playing: "Very little conscious thought happens when I'm playing drums. I strategize about the big picture, but when I'm playing, whatever happens, it's 'que sera, sera.'"

JAZZ

The son of a jazz musician turned American spy, Stewart grew up around jazz. He began taking drum lessons at age twelve, and he was almost immediately playing in bands. Buddy Rich was Stewart's early favorite drummer. At a young age he also took a liking to Sandy Nelson, about whom he says "'Let There Be Drums' gives him a deserved place in history, just from that one track." The rest of Nelson's recordings didn't hold up for Stewart, but someone who did was Karen Carpenter. "I saw a YouTube clip of Karen Carpenter kicking ass. Why did they hire a session guy?" The guy, of course, was Hal Blaine. Stewart felt Carpenter had a vibe that should not have been replaced, no matter the legendary status of Blaine.

After The Police achieved worldwide success, Stewart saw the Buddy Rich Big Band at Ronnie Scott's in London, and counts among his proudest achievements giving his father, Miles, the chance to meet and hang with Buddy at the show. While Stewart signed autographs for the young band members—all Police fans—Miles and Buddy, "old jazzers of the same vintage," talked about club owners, bandleaders, venues and the like. He also recalls with great pride Buddy approaching him at the Grammy awards to obtain an autograph for his young daughter Cathy. Not many drummers have given Buddy Rich their autograph.

The other major jazz drummers that Stewart heard through his dad at a young age were not drummers that he listened to regularly, although he cites Joe Morello as being someone he greatly admired. "'Take Five' is still a religious moment for me," he says. "When it comes on the radio, all conversation must stop. It is one of the most sublime uses of a drum set ever. I later came to appreciate Ed Thigpen, Philly Joe Jones, and Jo Jones because of the fire of what they did, but I was too young to really get them as a kid."

When asked about respecting Buddy Rich but being drawn into the world of rock music, Stewart takes a historical perspective: "There was an even bigger cultural watershed between my generation and that of my father than there was between, say, hippie fans and punk fans. My father's generation was the 'greatest generation' who fought the war, and the word 'teenager' was invented for my generation: the Baby Boomers. Between these generations, there was a cultural divide where much more had changed than in later shifts. It was short hair to long hair, and musically, it was saxophones to guitar. Later, between hippie and punk, it was the same instruments, same 100-watt amplifiers, same E, A and D chords—everything except attitude. All that changed was the hairdo. But between my father and me, it was jazz to rock, a much wider divide."

Stewart goes on to point out, correctly, that this divide "immunized" him from jazz because kids of his day didn't share any musical or cultural tastes or experience with their parents. What they were into was just too different—unlike today where kids might listen to Led Zeppelin or Buddy Rich with their parents. Stewart feels this is a major reason he never got deeply into jazz, and why kids today might be more exposed to it than he was.

ROCK

Most of Stewart's early exposure to music came during his teenage years while living in Beirut. Eager to get their hands on American music and culture, Stewart and his friends bought records at the one record store in Beirut's Ras Beirut section that sold Western music. Popular with the American kids, the store sold the Beatles, the Stones, the Kinks; and the BBC and the Voice of America had pop shows each week, which exposed a young Stewart to English and American music. He and his friends were desperate for any American culture they could get, and in his first band (the Black Knights), Stewart played songs by James Brown, the Kinks, Them (Van Morrison's early band) and more.

Copeland family home, Beirut, Lebanon (Photo courtesy Stewart Copeland).

Stewart and brother Ian, Beirut, Lebanon (Photo courtesy Stewart Copeland).

As far as the rock drummers that inspired Stewart the most in his early drumming days, it was Mitch Mitchell and Ginger Baker. Among fusion bands and drummers, Stewart appreciated Return to Forever and the Mahavishnu Orchestra with the great Billy Cobham.

REGGAE

Reggae became an influence for Stewart later. His family moved to the UK around 1966, when he was 14, and he went to boarding school in Somerset while his parents lived in London. It was at this time that he heard reggae for the first time. He cites the 1968 song "The Israelites," by Desmond Dekker, as having a huge impact on him. However, it wasn't until his college years, where he was a DJ at University of California at Berkeley, that he became

Stewart playing drums, Beirut, Lebanon (Photo courtesy Stewart Copeland).

familiar with the music. Bob Marley's "Lively Up Yourself," released in 1971, found Stewart gravitating towards the music, but without really analyzing the rhythms. He got into the vibe of it and loved the bass lines. Eventually he did start to analyze the drumming and realized it was quite different than any other style he was used to.

Back in London after college, Stewart was playing other music, "But when Don Letts started playing hostile dub in the punk clubs of London in 1976 and 1977," he says, "I started to analyze and wonder how to play reggae rhythms." He recalls the drummers Terry Chimes and Topper Headon of the Clash experimenting with reggae rhythms, and felt their use of the style had attitude, even if not the groove. Stewart never played in a reggae band. His

innate familiarity with the Arabic rhythms of his childhood made reggae feel natural to him, and he developed a unique approach that was colored by a hybridization of the Middle Eastern and reggae rhythms together.

Stewart and his fellow musicians heard a lot of dub reggae, because it was used to create a lull in the mood at the London punk clubs: "The DJs played dub reggae because you needed a moment of chill, and punks don't make chill music. The dub was slow and chill, but still pissed off. It was still angry, dark and hostile. It kept the mood of hostility simmering while they rested for a minute, you know, when the glue wore off."

COMPOSITION

Returning to the U.S. for college, Stewart first attended the United States International University in San Diego, studying music, and then went on to the University of California at Berkley, but did not major in music there. He recalls a story about the impact one of his teachers had on him at music school. "The chords for 'Does Everyone Stare' were a music theory exercise in figured bass. The exercise was to write sixteen bars with proper voice leading and such. During music school, I had not been doing my ear training but instead figuring out riffs and chords, but I couldn't actually join them together (in the way I was hearing). So I took what I was working on, and for this exercise I put them together with proper voice leading. In the class, I was the runt of the litter. I hadn't started on piano at age seven like everyone else in there, and I was struggling to keep up. The teacher played everyone's exercises, and when she came to mine, she played it through. She said, 'Well, you've got parallel fifths there, and that's not proper voice leading, but I see why you did it. In fact, Stewart, this is actual music.' That changed my life.

"I found that teacher later, and by that time I was a film composer and everything, but she couldn't remember me. But I remembered her. I guess she couldn't remember me because I was getting Cs and Ds in the back of the class. When I went to U.C. Berkeley, I couldn't get into the music school because I was not qualified, and my ear training wasn't up to scratch. I learned music theory at my previous college in San Diego, and then at Berkeley I majored in mass communications and public policy, which was actually much more useful (for a career in rock 'n' roll). None of my competitors in the Clash, the Jam, or the Damned knew any of that shit: how newspapers worked, how decisions are made by news editors about what is or isn't news, how radio works. It was like sociology combined with journalism and several other disciplines which were much more useful for a life in show business."

EARLY BANDS: CURVED AIR

Stewart played with progressive rock band Curved Air from 1975-76. His recollections are as follows: "I joined during the dregs at the end of the band's run. My buddy Mick Jacques joined on guitar; he was a blues guitarist and only wanted to play the blues. Years later I asked him what fuck he was doing in Curved Air! But he was a great guy, great player, very charismatic, and sort of a natural leader,

so we all followed him. So Curved Air almost became his blues band! But I was there during that fateful transition. We should have been listening more closely to Darryl Way, the violinist, because he was the prog guy, but, yeah, there were a lot of triplets."

Did Stewart listen to the prog bands of the day? He cites ELP, for example, as a group of musicians he respected, "without necessarily reaching for their albums. Kind of like Sandy Nelson, I went back and listened to their first album and wondered what I originally liked about it, and realized it was the heavy keyboard sound, and Carl Palmer's interesting rhythms. Jon Hiseman and Bob Henrit were heroes, and I respected Bill Bruford. He was the man. I read a celebrity review written by Buddy Rich where he said Bill had 'good hands.' So Bruford became *the shit*, because he had the blessing and dispensation from the pope of drums, Buddy himself!"

LONDON SCENE

Stewart formed The Police in 1976 with Sting on bass and vocals, and Henry Padovani on guitar. When Sting moved to London from Newcastle, Stewart took him out on the scene. The Roxy on Neal Street had recently opened, and there they saw Generation X, the Heartbreakers, and the Damned. All of these bands, and others, were playing all around town, and they all knew each other. According to Stewart, they all went to each other's gigs. "We were getting torn to shreds by the critics, who recognized us as carpetbaggers right away," says Stewart. "We were about five years older than most of the other bands, and more experienced as musicians. But while that was happening, the guys from other bands, like Joe Strummer, were coming to our gigs and copping licks from us. The critics were right, of course: We were flying a flag of convenience. In fact, after Andy joined the band, at our first gig Miles (Stewart's brother and the manager of The Police) noticed that Andy had cut his hair—but he hadn't turned in his bell bottoms! I laugh about this because I was the 'punk Nazi' of the band. Andy and Sting were just musicians, and I was always screaming that we had to fit into this (punk) mold so we could get shows. There weren't any shows for non-punk bands."

PART 2
THE POLICE

May 29, 1979; Munich, Germany, TV show shoot (Photo courtesy of Dietmar Clös).

THE POLICE EARLY YEARS

Stewart started to form The Police in late 1976. He used his brother Miles' resources, such as his office and contacts, to do business, because in the early days Stewart managed the band and made most decisions on his own, right down to choosing photos and using Letraset to create the artwork for posters, concert flyers and record sleeves.

Having a punk image was the key to getting gigs. Because none of their music was on the radio, punks would go into record stores and buy albums and singles based on the images of the band on the cover. Did it look hostile? Then they wanted it! "So that was my function in the band," Stewart laughs, "and then Sting and Andy started writing actual *songs* and getting all *musical.* They'd complain about me enforcing the punk thing." Interestingly, gigs were few and far between in the early days, and many came due to cancelations from other bands. They'd even play under the billing of other bands. "Many of these other bands were real kids," Stewart relates. "They sometimes couldn't get to the gig. They didn't know about professional responsibility, and that this is a job, and you have to show up. That was kind of antithetical to the 'stance.' So we did shows, but not that often. Mostly we rehearsed, and made a couple of records, which sold a couple thousand. The record stores sent me the checks. I remember putting the checks in the bank and then splitting the money three ways. A thousand records was a hit. I still have the receipts and my accounting books."

Around this time, the musicians of The Police, being in a starving punk band, did recording sessions for other artists to earn a living. One of the records they made at the time is by the band Strontium 90, fronted by Mike Howlett (released 20 years later with the title *Police Academy*). Howlett was dating Sting's music publisher, and he was the bass player in the band Gong. Howlett wanted two bass players on the recording, and called Sting, who brought Stewart as the drummer to the session. The guitarist on the session was Andy Summers, who was a well-known and respected studio musician in London. After making the album, Strontium 90 did one show at a Gong reunion concert in Paris, and then two gigs in London (under the name "The Elevators") where they filled time by playing some Police songs, which Andy had learned. At the next Police gig (at the Marquee in London), Andy came onstage to play, which resulted in him joining The Police. What is interesting is that this recording occurred during the time that The Police were keeping themselves restricted to a punk vocabulary, not allowing themselves to play anything that would call for technical chops. On *Police Academy*, Stewart, Sting and Andy can be heard stretching out their chops in a way they were not doing in The Police at the time.

Clockwise from top left: June 10, 1979; Lyceum Ballroom, L⟨

1979; Guildford, UK. June 10, 1979; Lyceum Ballroom, London. June 10, 1979; Lyceum Ballroom, London. All photos courtesy Dietmar Clös.

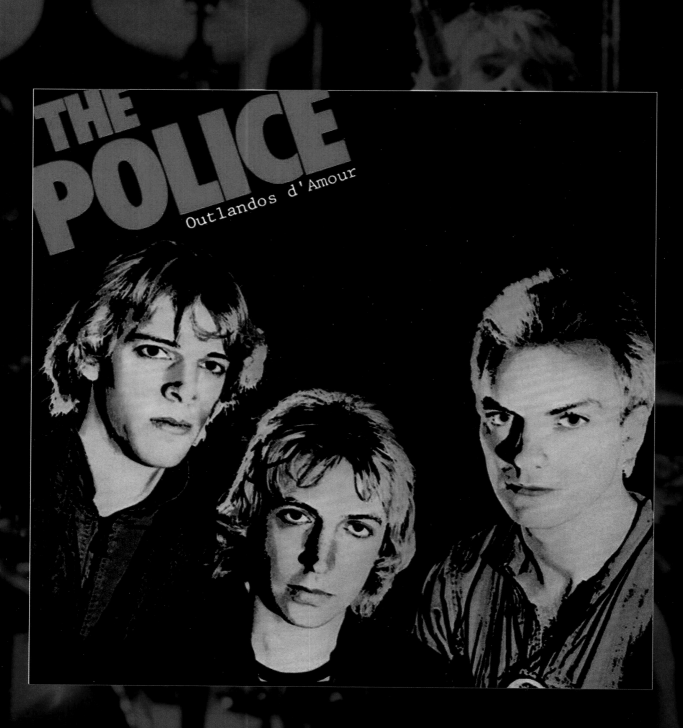

The first Police album was recorded between January and September, 1978. The band was busy doing gigs, playing the material that wound up on the album. When Miles Copeland heard "Roxanne," he suggested the band follow this direction with Sting's songwriting, so they got rid of some faster songs and re-recorded others. The album was finished around September 20, 1978. "Surrey Sound was a big room above a dairy," says Stewart. "*Outlandos D'Amour* was different than later Police records in that we knew the songs before we went into the studio. On the other albums, we never heard the songs until we were in the studio, with the tape rolling. On *Outlandos*, we worked out those songs, played shows with them, and had a chance to think about them, so it was kind of a different process than the other albums." English rock duo Godley & Creme were recording at Surrey during the day, so The Police came in at night over the course of six weeks to record *Outlandos*. According to Stewart, they bonded with the other musicians working at the studio.

Every Police album has a clear and crisp drum sound, starting with their first record. As producer, Nigel Gray of course had an impact on that sound, Stewart says, and captured the drums quite well. In addition to his engineering chops, Nigel was a good band referee, keeping the vibe smooth between the members. The snare drum sound on *Outlandos* is not extremely high-pitched like the later Police records, but it is higher than many records of the same period. When Stewart recorded with Curved Air, the producers suggested he play with a "fatback" sound of a deep snare played far behind the beat, which Stewart hated. He loved the fact that with The Police, no producer or engineer (whether Nigel Gray or Hugh Padgham) ever told him how to tune or play his drums.

Stewart's signature cross-stick sound was influenced by reggae drummers, as was his propensity for hitting the snare drum at the edge to get a ringy rim shot. "It was the opposite of fatback," says Stewart, "so I loved it. Reggae drummers played their chops all throughout the songs; they didn't wait until the end of every sixteen bars. I stole as many (of their ideas) as I could." Getting from the normal snare stroke to the cross-stick position is something that Stewart says was always a challenge. Being a traditional grip player, he would turn his hand over and play the cross-stick with the butt end of the stick.

"Roxanne," like many Police tracks, has a groove approach that does not always use a backbeat. While it sounds like it has a reggae influence, Stewart points out that many of the details are not authentic or "correct" reggae concepts. It was the mix of the Arabic baladi rhythms—absorbed during his childhood in the Middle East—with his later rock, jazz, and reggae concepts that created Stewart's unique "stew" of grooves. The non-Western rhythms gave him a full range of timekeeping options that didn't require two and

November 25, 1978: Electric Ballroom, London (Courtesy of Dietmar Clös).

June 11, 1979: Guildford, UK (Courtesy of Dietmar Clös).

four on the snare. In turn, this meant Stewart could craft drum parts that could change feel and drive with different sections of a song whenever he so desired. In the construction of his drum parts, Stewart's philosophy is best described as composition combined with improvisation. He would have an overall strategy for the drum part, but would improvise freely within that framework, so that fills, for instance, were always improvised.

ROXANNE

An iconic Police track, "Roxanne" was released as a single ahead of the full *Outlandos D'Amour* album, but it did not chart. Sting originally wrote the song as a bossa nova, but Stewart suggested changing the rhythmic form to what you hear on the final track. Stewart's compositional sense is evident in the song as he changes the density and intensity of the drum part to match the sections of the song. The intro is sparse, with a snare backbeat only on beat 2 of each bar. In the verses he adds the second backbeat of the bar, and then a tom-tom to accentuate the end of the bar as the verse repeats. The chorus is louder and much more intense, with driving bass drum underneath the backbeats.

The second half of the second verse contains use of the ride bell as Stewart improvises accents to create texture while playing the snare/tom groove. This type of phrasing is one of Stewart's musical signatures and appears across all his playing. The driving chorus of the song contains the energy and spirit of punk music, as does much of the rest of this album.

ROXANNE

ROXANNE

ROXANNE

Chorus 2

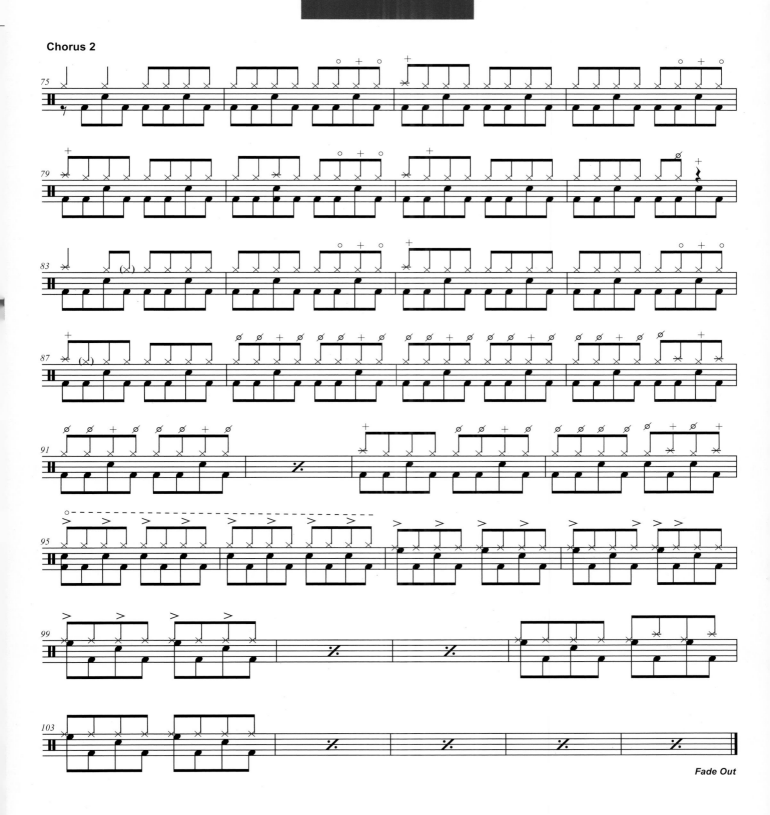

Fade Out

CAN'T STAND LOSING YOU

Like "Roxanne," "Can't Stand Losing You" displays many of the drumming techniques Stewart would employ on later recordings.

It opens with a straight-four bass drum pattern and eighth notes on the hi-hat, which Stewart uses frequently as a device to create drive without the volume and intensity of a full backbeat groove. The verse resembles "Roxanne" in that the drums allow space by leaving out a backbeat, except in this case the backbeat on 2 is omitted. Layering the toms in with the snare drum creates a pitched motif in the groove.

The pre-chorus and chorus have a punk-like drive, especially the pre-chorus with its sloshy hi-hats. The chorus features a ride pattern that accentuates quarter notes on the bell. In the middle interlude of the song, there are some syncopated cross-stick rhythms. Stewart would develop this concept highly on later songs. In the final chorus of the song, a tom is again layered into the groove to create more drive.

Notice how the drum part relies on texture and creativity within the grooves. The fills in the song are simple and minimal; the energy and interest is created within the grooves.

CAN'T STAND LOSING YOU

CAN'T STAND LOSING YOU

CAN'T STAND LOSING YOU

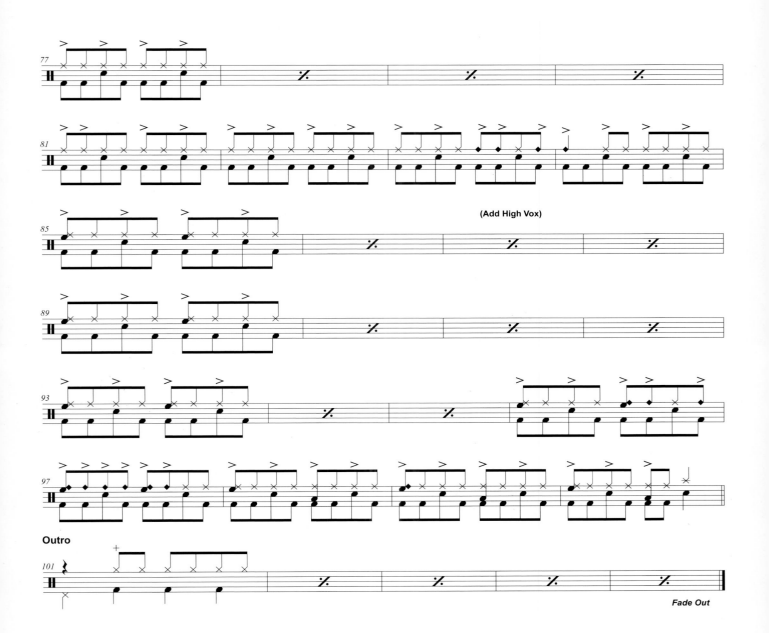

(Add High Vox)

Outro

Fade Out

Clockwise from top left:

June 10, 1979: Lyceum Ballroom, London (© Craig Betts).

June 22, 1979: Paradiso, Amsterdam (Courtesy of Dietmar Clös).

June 23, 1979: Sankt Goarshausen, Germany 1979 (Courtesy of Dietmar Clös).

March 8, 1979: Houston, TX (Courtesy Dietmar Clös).

June 10, 1979: London Lyceum (Courtesy of Dietmar Clös).

REGGATTA DE BLANC

Following the recording of *Outlandos d'Amour*, The Police went on tour. Stewart relates the story: "Miles and Ian had figured out how to export U.K. punk to America. My brother Ian, who was an agent at the time down in Macon, Georgia, for Southern rock bands, created a circuit. On Tuesday, the Rat in Boston; on Wednesday, Grendel's Lair in Philadelphia; and then CBGB and Max's Kansas City in New York. Of course, New York being New York, it already had a scene, but he exported that scene to other cities. On this circuit he created, the first U.K. band was Squeeze, for whom Miles and Ian bought a station wagon and a couple of amps, and Gil brought his drums over as hand luggage. Squeeze caught a flight back to London just as we arrived, and we picked up the same van and amps, and I brought my drums as hand luggage, and we played CBGB.

"I got to New York a day early, and being American, I got right in, but the other guys were held up due to visas and got in the night of our show at CBGB. Miles went and picked them up and drove them right from the airport to the club, which was a shithole, and they plugged into some amps they had never seen before, turned around, and it was 'hello, America!' And so began the conquest. While we were doing these early tours, the singles from *Outlandos* began to catch."

When the band came back to Surrey Sound to finish their second album (during July and August of 1979), they were short of material. "We hadn't even written a full album," says Stewart. "A lot of the material was put together in the studio." Sting, not being a collaborative writer, didn't reveal a lot of what he was working on, although Stewart remembers a few new things being played at soundchecks.

Stewart began to use overdubs and digital delay much more prominently on this album. The amount of drum set overdubbing, as opposed to adding a lot of percussion instruments, is rare among rock drummers. "I wasn't trying to add groove, like adding a conga or tambourine part," said Stewart about his general use of drum set overdubs. "I was adding punctuation; something to enhance an existing groove, like adding a ride cymbal bell to accent with an existing snare. If something didn't punch or lift enough, I would add dynamic."

On this album, as on all the following Police albums, the recording of the basic tracks was split up, where the initial sessions were only to capture the final performances on the drums, with the rest of the parts being replaced later. "It was the same with all the bands of that period," says Stewart. "The drummer had to get his shit together first, then everyone else had the luxury of going in there later, worrying about which guitar pickup to use. And then once the drummer was finished recording, he was told to go play Space Invaders, because the musicians were at work here now!"

Because The Police had ultimately turned a profit from the sales and tour from *Outlandos d'Amour*, they were able to pay for the recording of *Reggatta* themselves, and therefore there was really no influence on the music or recording by their record company, A&M.

From left: September 22, 1979; Hammersmith Odeon, London (photos 1 & 2 courtesy of Dietmar Clös). Hammersmith Odeon, London, December 18, 1979 (photo © Craig Betts).

MESSAGE IN A BOTTLE

Stewart recorded the basic track for this song and then went back and added overdubs on the kit. In the recording process, Stewart and the band (and producer) would listen to a take, and if they liked a certain performance but it needed more lift or punctuation, Stewart would go back out to the drums and overdub on top of that take. Some of these overdub ideas came from Stewart, while some were suggested by Andy or Sting. When asked about whether he worried about reproducing these parts live, Stewart suggests "somehow the physical presence and the energy of a live show replaces what might be lost in terms of overdubs." Stewart mentions Trevor Horn and Jeff Lynne as performers who might recreate a recording note-for-note onstage, but he doesn't feel the same need to do so. Stewart humorously refers to this as "disloyalty to the canon." "It never occurred to us—this idea of fans bonding with the recordings—and part of why I probably never thought about it is because I arrived at the parts so frivolously. It was stuff I just made up five minutes ago! Unlike Neil Peart, I didn't compose the parts. I had a general strategy, but all the little details that fans sometimes obsess over were spontaneous, and they were completely different on the next take. We didn't think of recreating the recording onstage; we thought about recreating the *band* onstage as our philosophy."

This song is a great example of a kind of "signature strategy" Stewart employs: a sparse groove, often missing the downbeat of "1" alongside a four-on-the-floor ska-ish section and then a driving rock groove, usually saving "2 and 4" on the snare drum for the choruses. The intro is a driving snare flam pattern with hi-hat overdubbed on top for the first four bars. For the verses, Stewart overdubbed a ride cymbal bell on top of the snare drum backbeats, and in the pre-chorus and second verse there are tom overdubs. There is also a woodblock or temple block sparsely dropped in during the choruses. From time to time, Stewart had cowbells or temple blocks in his setup, and they appeared in places like this. There are some interesting hi-hat syncopations with stabbing crashes in measures 83-98.

The final mix of the song makes it difficult to tell what was played in the main take and what was overdubbed, so transcriber Mike Sorrentino and I asked Stewart about it, and he revealed that it is actually the backbeats that are overdubbed in the latter half of the song. "I definitely did overdub snare at the end," says Stewart. "There was too much sprangle, so we laid a backbeat all down the outro. I regret the mess at the end of an otherwise good recording. The basic part (i.e., the 2 & 4 backbeat) was the overdub!"

Note: For this chart, the overdubs are written on a second staff for clarity. The standard drum key applies to both staves.

MESSAGE IN A BOTTLE

MESSAGE IN A BOTTLE

Pre Chorus 1

Chorus 1

MESSAGE IN A BOTTLE

Verse 2

Pre Chorus 2

Chorus 2

Block

Verse 3

MESSAGE IN A BOTTLE

Chorus 3

Block

Reprise

MESSAGE IN A BOTTLE

Outro

MESSAGE IN A BOTTLE

Fade Out

WALKING ON THE MOON

This song features a famous delay line on the drums. Stewart used delay on many tracks, but this one is probably best known. (For another excellent example, listen to the title track of the same album, "Reggatta de Blanc.") "I can remember Nigel Gray being really excited about the sound of the delay," Stewart recalls. Gray generated the delay effect for this song in the studio. When the delay is engaged, one echo of each note is produced. The overlaying delayed notes create the dense audio effect on this song. The delayed notes occur a dotted eighth note after the played note, creating a more polyrhythmic effect than an eighth-note delay (which would have more delayed notes overlapping with played ones, such as on "Every Little Thing She Does is Magic").

While the delay on the *Reggatta* album was created in the studio, Stewart developed a way to produce it live soon thereafter. "One day in New York City on the *Reggatta* tour, we got a call saying 'Boys, the money has dropped. You are now rich!' So we went down to Manny's on 48th Street and bought *everything*. We said, 'We'll take that chorus, that echo, that Jazz Chorus amp, that Stratocaster, those Taurus pedals—we just bought everything in the store. Our show that night (Oct 2, 1979) was at My Father's Place on Long Island, and it was the soundcheck from hell, because of all the new gear. The guys were playing with their new toys, mostly from Roland (who was the flavor of the month), and my new toys were for my guitar playing, not my drums.

"Dub was a thing, as I said before, because of the hostile dub thing where you click delay lines off and on. Later on, Jeff Seitz hooked me up a foot pedal so I could turn on chorus echo, and I was doing live dub. Jeff and I were really excited about that. I was playing with my delay lines through my new Roland Jazz Chorus amp, because I wasn't elevated to the dignity of actually going through the P.A. with this bullshit—that came later! At that soundcheck was where I discovered that trick of the echo, and the rest of the tour was full of it."

The basic concept Stewart used for the delay in many cases was that the repeated note would fall a dotted eighth note behind the note he played, creating a kind of shuffle. In "Walking on the Moon," the delayed note effectively falls on the last note of the triplet (if the played note occurred on the downbeat), or two triplet partials later. Thus, a note played on the last triplet partial would produce an echo on the middle partial of the next triplet. This effect is turned on and off various parts of the drum set throughout the song, most notably on the snare drum cross-stick.

Note: All of the notes produced by the delay, whether on kick, snare, or hi-hat, are represented by a serifed "x" in parentheses. While this makes the chart harder to read, it documents the rhythms Stewart created by interacting with the delay, which is something he wanted us to document with this chart. To get what he actually played, omit the notes in parentheses.

WALKING ON THE MOON

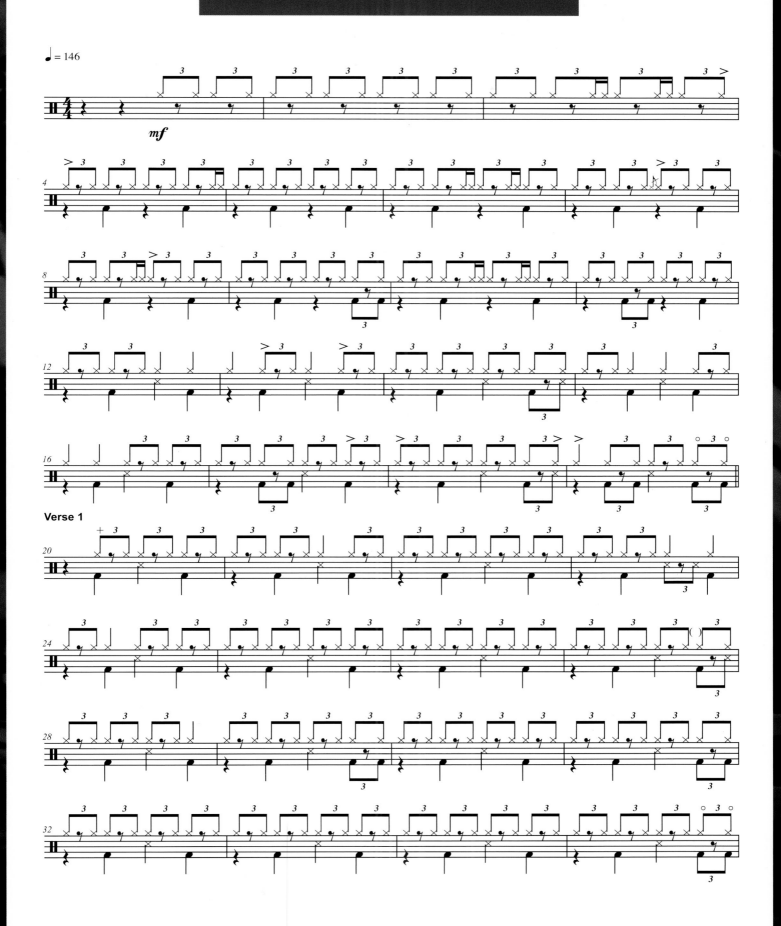

WALKING ON THE MOON

WALKING ON THE MOON

WALKING ON THE MOON

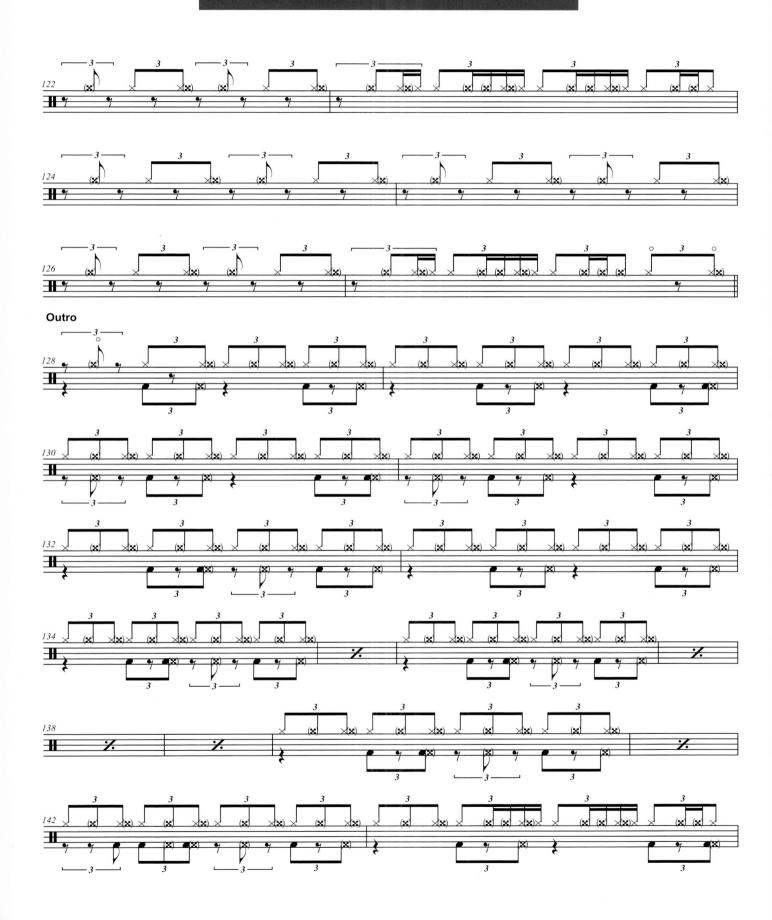

Outro

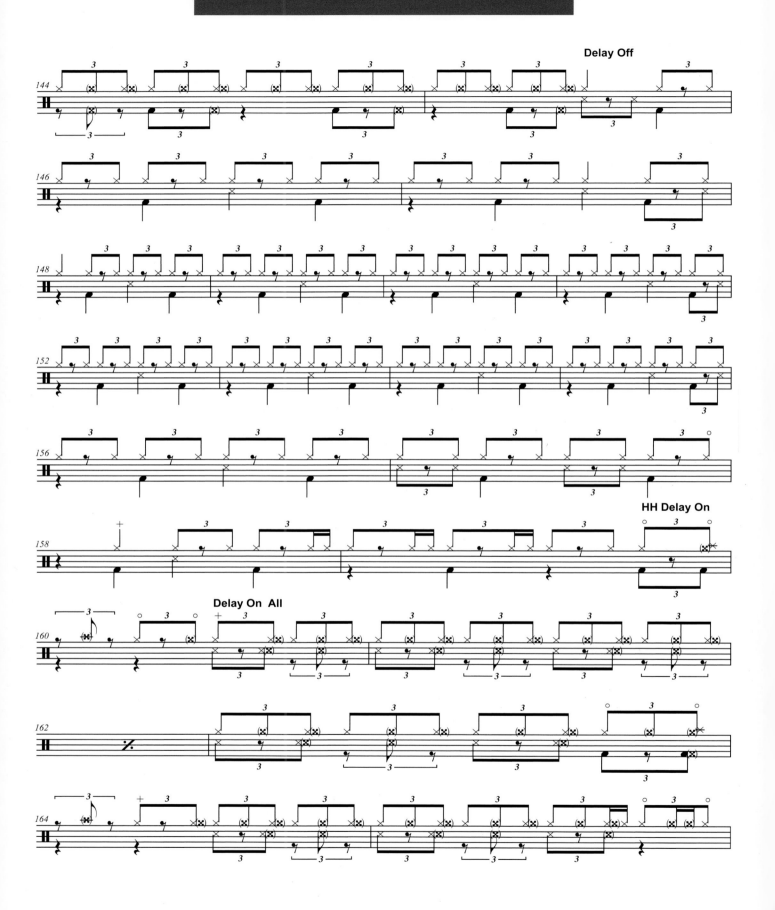

WALKING ON THE MOON

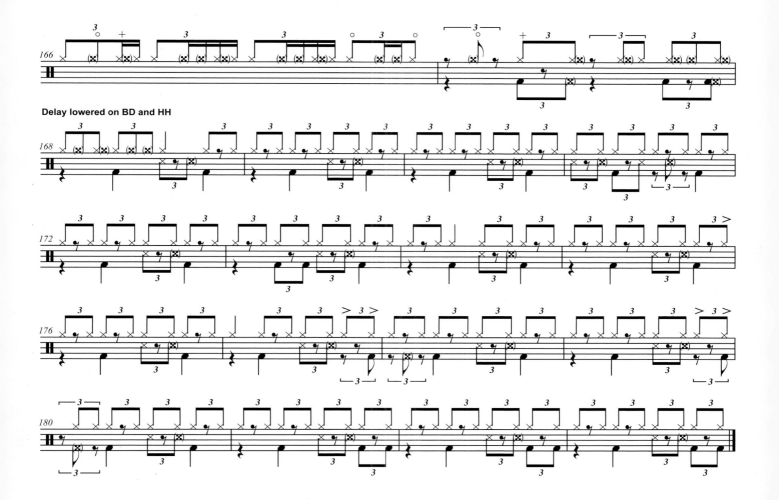

Delay lowered on BD and HH

ZENYATTA MONDATTA

Zenyatta Mondatta was recorded during July and August 1980 at Wisseloord Studios in the Netherlands, with Nigel Gray once again co-producing. The switch to recording outside of England was for tax reasons, and the sessions took place during a frenetic time. "We left the studio and took off on tour," said Stewart, "and then interrupted the tour to do some mixing back in England, then went right back on tour again. It was kind of rushed, and it was the toughest because it was our breakthrough. We were told that if we cracked this third album, we'd be worldwide." Unlike the first two albums, the band was under a lot of pressure to produce a hit. "We felt the pressure, and the record company people were there in our face," relates Stewart. "We had record company executives sitting at the mixing board asking, 'Is that the hit?' Consequently, our next album was recorded twelve hours flight from the nearest record executive! So there was a lot of pressure on us. The most would be on Sting, as the songwriter, and he totally delivered. We kind of had that feature: When the pressure was the highest, the band seemed to step up. The most pressurized shows were our best shows."

At the same time, Stewart didn't hear the songs he'd be recording until they were actually in the studio and Sting brought in his new material. Therefore, the final performances on the record are very soon after Stewart first heard and learned the songs. Still, they didn't do very many takes. "We usually did about three takes," says Stewart, "and the second one was usually it. We'd start getting bored, and the other guys wanted to start having some fun overdubbing their parts. By this time, Sting had perfected his technique of revealing the songs only one at a time. He would reveal a song, we'd chew on it for twenty or thirty minutes, and then start doing takes." The "working up" of the songs was an informal process with Sting and Andy playing their guitars acoustically and Stewart "slapping his thighs."

The quick work process of learning and recording the songs sometimes had unexpected results in the drum parts. "Sometimes I'd record what I thought was the verse-chorus-verse-chorus arrangement of the song, but Sting's verse would have two more lines—so I'd already be in the chorus, but he was still in the verse." There were basic guide vocals, but not enough to represent the final vocal. The result was that some of the transitions between sections in the drum parts were "accidental" in this regard.

Jeff Seitz relates the craziness of this period: "I set him up for *Zenyatta* and then went home to go on a summer vacation. My family was dissolving because I had been on the road for five months, and then it got back together when I got off the tour, so I decided to go away with them for two weeks. I drove the equipment van to the studio (in the Netherlands), set (the gear) up, drove back to London and flew home. Then I came back, picked up the gear, and we went on to do a couple of shows in Dublin, Ireland and Milton Keynes, UK. Then they went back in the studio to finish up some stuff, and then we went on a big French tour. Miles and the agents had set up the tour. They (the band) didn't like to muck around in the studio anyway, they went in and got it done. Actually, for this tour they rehearsed in the studio. They brought in the monitor engineer and got it all set up. Stewart was set up in a little drum booth which was open to the rest of the studio. Andy was somewhere else and Sting was usually in the control room."

Tama provided Stewart with a new kit for this album, a mahogany-colored Superstar. The drum sound on the record is really out front in the mix, and the tones are crisp. This is the first album on which Stewart used his newly-acquired Pearl snare, and it is cranked to a very high tension. Stewart preferred the sound of the Tama Imperialstar drums, so *Zenyatta* is the only album on which the Superstar kit appears. It is now in the possession of Jeff Seitz, who still uses it from time to time.

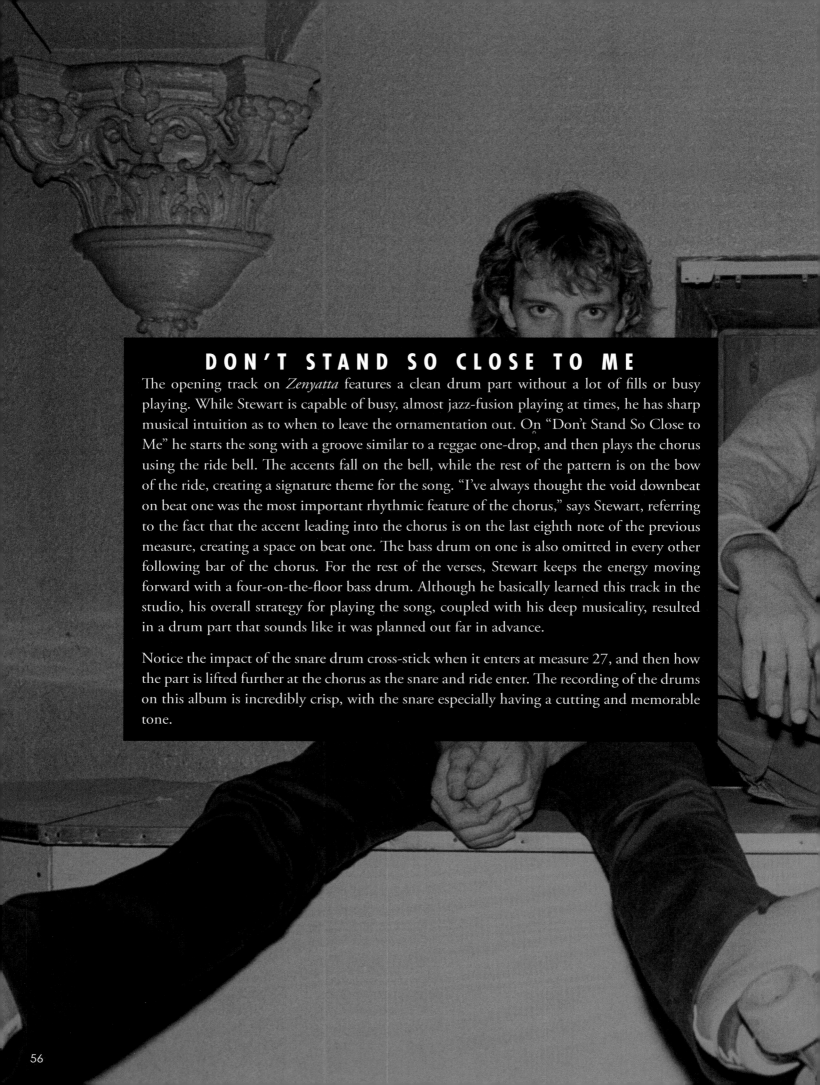

DON'T STAND SO CLOSE TO ME

The opening track on *Zenyatta* features a clean drum part without a lot of fills or busy playing. While Stewart is capable of busy, almost jazz-fusion playing at times, he has sharp musical intuition as to when to leave the ornamentation out. On "Don't Stand So Close to Me" he starts the song with a groove similar to a reggae one-drop, and then plays the chorus using the ride bell. The accents fall on the bell, while the rest of the pattern is on the bow of the ride, creating a signature theme for the song. "I've always thought the void downbeat on beat one was the most important rhythmic feature of the chorus," says Stewart, referring to the fact that the accent leading into the chorus is on the last eighth note of the previous measure, creating a space on beat one. The bass drum on one is also omitted in every other following bar of the chorus. For the rest of the verses, Stewart keeps the energy moving forward with a four-on-the-floor bass drum. Although he basically learned this track in the studio, his overall strategy for playing the song, coupled with his deep musicality, resulted in a drum part that sounds like it was planned out far in advance.

Notice the impact of the snare drum cross-stick when it enters at measure 27, and then how the part is lifted further at the chorus as the snare and ride enter. The recording of the drums on this album is incredibly crisp, with the snare especially having a cutting and memorable tone.

DON'T STAND SO CLOSE TO ME

DON'T STAND SO CLOSE TO ME

DON'T STAND SO CLOSE TO ME

Chorus

Fade Out

From top: *Zenyatta Mondatta* session, Wisseloord Studios, Netherlands,1980 (Photo by Danny Quatrochi). November 9, 1979: Police at the Riviera Theater in Chicago, Illinois (Photo by Paul Natkin).

DRIVEN TO TEARS

This track showcases many of Stewart's signature drumming concepts. Most noticeable is his mastery of the use of accents to color the part, both on the hi-hat and on the ride cymbal. He breaks up the placement of notes and accents to add variety and a sense of urgency to the driving, underlying quarter-note ska bass drum pulse. The chorus switches to a half-time backbeat on the snare, with all kinds of little accents and toys coloring the groove. The icebell, octobans, splashes and toms are used in an exciting yet tasteful way.

Listen to the various shades of accents on hi-hat and ride, and the phrasing of his fills, sometimes moving across the bar lines. Stewart had a funny commentary on his improvisational approach to his drum parts. Regarding his "strategy" of using non-backbeat/Arabic/reggae concepts for the verses and saving the backbeat for the choruses, he replies, "I'll go with that word 'strategy,' because I do have a strategy. What I lack is tactics. What I do when I get to it is all fucked up. But there is indeed a strategy."

DRIVEN TO TEARS

Clockwise from top left: November 7, 1980, Phoenix, AZ (Photo by Lissa Wales). *Zenyatta Mondatta* tour (Photo by Danny Quatrochi).
September 1980, Covent Garden, London (© Craig Betts). May 1980, Clapham, London (© Craig Betts).
Left: November 27, 1979, A&M Records, NYC (© Craig Betts).

THE **POLICE**

GHOST IN THE MACHINE

GHOST IN THE MACHINE

For *Ghost in the Machine*, The Police recorded on the Caribbean island of Montserrat, in an effort to have a more private environment away from record company personnel. The sessions were not without stress, however. "We've never been a cuddling band," says Stewart. "We've always been confrontational, and we each set high standards for the *other* guys. I've often described The Police as a Prada suit made out of barbed wire."

Ghost in the Machine and *Synchronicity* were co-produced by Hugh Padgham, and the drum sound on both albums is legendary. Both were recorded at AIR Studios on Montserrat. "They (The Police) asked XTC how they liked their producer (Steve Lilywhite), because they liked the sound of their records," remembers Jeff Seitz. "XTC said, 'You don't need Steve, you need his engineer.' So that's how they hired Hugh. His detail of miking the drums and not saturating the tape were key. A lot of people would redline the kick drum, but Hugh knew you'd be losing transients at that point already, so he was always at like minus 20 on the analog meters. His use of room mics with compression, to give it that crunchy sound, and gates as well" added to the groundbreaking sound.

"The biggest thing with Hugh, was his breakthrough recording technique," says Stewart. "He created this whole concept of the ambient drum sound. He put the drums in the most ambient room he could find, which in the case of

Montserrat was the dining room of this big wooden building. He had the drums close miked, but he also had the compressed Neumanns way back in the room, which gave it that vibrant, amazing sound. Hugh also had a lot of great techniques about where to place the microphone to get the best sound not only from the drums, but also the guitar, bass, vocals, and everything. The downside is that I'm up in the dining room in a different building from the band, and I've got a monitor which shows me the control room. And I can see my two very grumpy colleagues (Sting and Andy) assuming the same position as the record company guys at Hilversum (Wisseloord for the *Zenyatta* sessions)." The result of all this was that after about three takes of each tune, Stewart was essentially finished with his track.

"By the way," he adds, "We had another drum set in the main room. The main room was full of guitars and amps—that was Andy's room. Sting was in the control room because he didn't need any other gear. I don't know if I used (this other drum set) for any recordings, but we shot some videos with it. (Note: This drum set is seen in the video for "Every Little Thing She Does is Magic.") I had the delay line gear in the room with me because we had evolved the technology. Jeff figured out a system where I could turn them on with my heel, so a lot of those things were recorded on the spot, as a separate audio line. This allowed me to interact with the slap-back as it was happening."

1982 - Photo by Lissa Wales.

Moving the drums up to the dining room was done because Hugh didn't like the sound of the studio. "Demolition Man" was done in the studio, but then Hugh decided to try moving the drums upstairs to improve the sound. The dining room had hardwood floors, high cathedral ceilings and glass windows all around. "I hit the snare once and said, 'Oh yeah, this is going to be good!'" recalls Seitz. Padgham was pleased with the sound, but he added sound baffles around the kit. "They ran mic cables out of the studio, up the patio stairs, and into the dining room," says Jeff. "They had to wrap all the cables because the monsoon rains would come and the cables were all sitting out there. The next year we came back, and they built a trough underneath the studio for the cables. The heat was brutal; Stewart was working his ass off. It was the humid tropics and there was no air conditioning upstairs." "It was very hot in the room, and I got kind of sick, and the doctor said I needed electrolytes," says Stewart. "They hadn't invented Gatorade yet, so I had to take electrolyte pills, which are basically salt."

SPIRITS IN THE MATERIAL WORLD

Right from the creative opening drum fill, the first track on *Ghost in the Machine* is driving and somewhat dark, with an infectious melody and groove. It's another great example of Stewart's compositional approach and how The Police adapted World music concepts into their songwriting formula. In the verses, Sting's active bass line carries the melody, and Andy Summers' upbeat guitar/synthesizer is reminiscent of reggae. The verse drum part hints at a non-Western feel without sounding exactly like any specific genre.

The drum part is disciplined in the sense of Stewart's decision to stick to the two basic grooves and ornament them only with a few variations in the hi-hat part. He plays mainly upbeats on the hats, but there are other accents, and the non-accented downbeats are also mostly played. This takes a surprising amount of hand technique to pull off smoothly. The "fill" leading into the choruses is one loud stroke on the snare to set up the backbeat groove. No crash cymbal is played in the song until after the last chorus, yet the energy and drive push forward relentlessly. Stewart's famous snare drum sound is on full display here, as well as his ultra-crisp hi-hat playing, and an occasional icebell accent. There is a super-cool, syncopated reggae fill that starts the song, which uses the small tom and snare (with the tom cranked up to jazz-drummer tightness).

Stewart describes this song and groove as "tightly wound but unadorned." This is a groove that exemplifies Stewart's exposure to Middle Eastern rhythms and reggae, coalescing them into his own style. "In a lot of the places where The Police grooves hit people as reggae," says Stewart, "I'm actually playing the Lebanese baladi (Arabic for "country") while Andy's guitar upbeats are right out of reggae, and Sting's bass lines have these big rhythmic 'black holes' (spaces) to fill up."

SPIRITS IN THE MATERIAL WORLD

Chorus 2

Interlude

mf

Verse 3

Ice Bell

Chorus 3

Fade Out

EVERY LITTLE THING SHE DOES IS MAGIC

Sting recorded the demo of this song on 16-track in Montreal with pianist Jean Roussel, and it is this demo that forms the base of track, as Stewart ultimately recorded over the demo to create the final version. This was not before they flew Roussel to Montserrat and tried to record the song from scratch. "Sting wrote this in Montreal, where he was hanging out with (Roussel), and together they concocted this song, and his piano was a big part of it," says Stewart. "He had this demo, and it was a hit as it was. It was like 'Release this demo and we've got another worldwide smash,' which was not a delight for Andy and me. So we tried everything: the punk version, the reggae version, a mellow version, and nothing was as good as the demo. And the extent to which we didn't replicate the demo made it that much further away from a bullseye hit, so finally I just overdubbed to the demo. The piano player did show up to the studio, much to the irritation of Andy: He (Jean) was soon tinkling away overdubbing on all the tracks, until Andy threw him out. I did get Andy's point; we were a guitar band and didn't want to become a four-piece, so out he went. But his piano parts did live on that track."

According to Seitz, "They put the 16-track tape up on the 24-track machine, which frees up extra tracks, because you can record in between the 16. Andy overdubbed guitars, and there were only a few tracks of drums. And they didn't do one take. They were dropping Stewart in. There was a rhythm box on the demo that he played along to."

Stewart pulls off his own magic with this track, accomplishing a rare feat: Recording a busy, "drummer's drummer" part on a song that became a monster hit. The verse groove builds from the beginning, starting with hi-hat and then adding cross-stick and bass drum. The density builds to the chorus, in which Stewart pulls a rainbow of colors out of the ride cymbal in measures 26-33, with various velocities of notes played on the bell and bow. While the fills were improvised, some, like the ones at measures 91 and 121, are considered "signature" parts in the song by drummers. Last but not least, pay close attention to Stewart's command of the hi-hat on this track. There are tasty touches all through the song: syncopated accents, embellishments, 16th-note triplets, and a bewildering variety of degrees of tight, loose or open hat sounds.

There is a delay used in this song. It echoes the hi-hat a sixteenth note after the played note. This has the result of causing many of the notes produced by the delay to overlap a note that is actually being played. When coupled with the different levels of accents that Stewart plays on the hi-hat, the result is a multi-layered, accented hi-hat part that sounds like two drummers playing a complementary part to one another. Aside from this, there is a short section near the end of the track where the ride bell was overdubbed. The drum part itself is exciting and busy, with the snare drum, hi-hat and ride being played in a way that explores and brings out multiple timbres on each instrument.

Note: the clearly audible accents produced by the delay are shown with a serifed "x" in parentheses. Measures 78-79 have delayed notes which have been left out for clarity, to show what was played.

EVERY LITTLE THING SHE DOES IS MAGIC

EVERY LITTLE THING SHE DOES IS MAGIC

EVERY LITTLE THING SHE DOES IS MAGIC

EVERY LITTLE THING SHE DOES IS MAGIC

Ride Cym Overdub

ONE WORLD (NOT THREE)

Created from an improvised jam, this song has an exciting drum part that varies between two basic drum grooves. Check out the intense energy and tight swing feel as he launches the tune with driving backbeats, then drops them out for a ska-type verse section with the kick on 1 and 3 (measure 10). He keeps this tension up for the whole song, switching between sections with backbeats and sections without them, connecting these grooves with jagged fills. Listen to the octobans setting up an over-the-bar-line transition at measure 33, and the syncopated icebell accents from measure 43-48. These really exemplify Stewart's creativity, sense of orchestration, and advanced use of syncopation.

Another interesting spot is the tom/crash fill at measure 89, after which he returns to 1-and-3 ska pattern but layers the snare over it. Measures 98-105 are another killer phrase, with driving ride-bell accents capped by a multi-voice fill including toms and splashes. Measures 148-171 are intense, with Stewart playing fills with abandon, incorporating octobans, toms, and varied rhythms including over-the-bar line implied quarter-note triplets. He then drops the drums out completely (except for foot hat) until he launches a busy snare fill at 179 and then a variation on the main groove to take the song out.

Regarding the various echoes and delays on this track, Stewart had the following to say: "Probably in the fullness of the process, we didn't use my live delay slapback. I'm pretty sure that Hugh would rather have recreated it with his higher-grade gear. What I had live was kind of freeform and not as efficient as what we would end up using later. So you might be hearing artifacts of what I had going on in the room, but I guess they were recreated later. And we used to gate everything as well."

Note: On the chart, we indicated clear and obvious spots where the delay effect creates additional notes, but it is engaged in some way for the whole track, and there are artifacts of tom/snare/octoban hits in various places that were probably triggered by the delay. There is an obvious delay engaged in measures 61-65 and 122-128, as noted. The hi-hat also has delay for almost the whole track; we attempted to notate what was played as accurately as possible.

ONE WORLD (NOT THREE)

ONE WORLD (NOT THREE)

ONE WORLD (NOT THREE)

ONE WORLD (NOT THREE)

ONE WORLD (NOT THREE)

Fade Out

Ghost in the Machine tour soundcheck, August 17, 1982, Nashville Municipal Auditorium (Photo by Jim Pettit).

Top: *Ghost in the Machine* recording session, Air Studios, Montserrat 1981 (Photo by Danny Quatrochi). Bottom: November 8, 1980, Tuscon, AZ (Photo by Lissa Wales).

Top: *Ghost in the Machine* sessions, Air Studios, Montserrat, B kit (Photo by Danny Quatrochi).

Left: Dallas, 1982 (Photo courtesy Dietmar Clös).

Opposite: *Ghost in the Machine* tour, 1982 (Photo by Danny Quatrochi).

SYNCHRONICITY

The final Police album was released in June 1983, and was a worldwide hit, selling over eight million copies, reaching #1 on the charts in the U.S. and U.K., and winning three Grammy awards. As with *Ghost in the Machine*, Hugh Padgham co-produced and engineered the album and it was recorded at AIR Studios in Montserrat, with Stewart in a separate room from the other band members. The rhythms on the album are a crystallization of the Arabian, reggae, punk and rock influences from the earlier albums with hints of other styles added to the mix. World music influences are present in "Tea in the Sahara" and "Walking in Your Footsteps," while the two "Synchronicity" tracks rock hard while employing a buoyancy created by Stewart's use of syncopation and the internal dynamics of his drumming. "Every Breath You Take" and "King of Pain" are master classes in pop songwriting, and "Murder by Numbers" has a 12/8 feel that has elements of jazz and blues.

Although the drums were recorded in the same room with the same method as *Ghost in the Machine*, the final tracks sound slightly different in tone. "After we finished *Synchronicity*, we went to mix it in Montreal," says Stewart. "The guys there said, 'There's this new technology… check this out!' and they ran our mix through PCM technology, which had just been invented, digitizing it. We thought, 'Wow, you can hear the space in between everything!' But what we now know is that it lost a lot of wave form. It created space but lost texture. (At the time) my buddy

Jeff Lynne was the lone voice raging against digitization."

The only Police songs recorded to an external tempo, according to Stewart, were "Synchronicity I" (which uses a sequenced keyboard part) and "Every Breath You Take," which was done to a click and had all the drums overdubbed. For that track, according to Jeff Seitz, the bass drum is an Oberheim drum machine kick, the backbeats are overdubbed with snare and gong drum together, and then the hi-hat and crash cymbals were also overdubbed separately. "'Every Breath You Take' was one of the songs that was very different in the process from everything else," says Stewart. "We tried a lot of different versions. The demo tape was a Hammond organ and vocals, which is obviously not much fun for Andy, so he worked out that arpeggiated guitar pattern from the Hammond. That's something Andy was very good at: achieving harmony, and his voicing is a big part of our sound. All the drums were recorded disparately. We started with an Oberheim drum box, and the part was so solid and fit perfectly—I would never have had the discipline to play that; it's hard enough live. We fought over the hi-hat: Sting wanted to use the Oberheim, but I had recorded my own (acoustic) hi-hat. I came back the next day and Sting had erased it and put the Oberheim back. On the record, Sting might think it's the Oberheim, but I have the multi-track. It's my hi-hat! The backbeat was a gong drum and a snare drum, with a gong drum crescendo into the chorus and a cymbal roll. I think

there was also an overdubbed ride cymbal bell. It was one of the few times I got to play with overdubs like everyone else!"

Regarding the function of Hugh Padgham and Nigel Gray, Stewart relates that neither producer had any input as to the actual parts that were being played; their focus as producers for The Police was to capture the sounds and performances, and to have (as Stewart put it) a good "bedside manner" to keep the band members working together with a minimum of tension.

By the time of the *Synchronicity* tour, The Police were the biggest band in the world. Jeff Seitz has fond memories. "It was a buzz, like a rocket ride. There was non-stop action, setting up, getting the show running, and then 25,000 or 30,0000 people in an arena or stadium. We were self-contained, there were three crew members plus the monitor guy, front of house guy, and lighting guy." Did Stewart feel more pressure as the band played for bigger and bigger audiences? "No, it got easier and easier," he says. "Playing an arena or stadium is easier than playing your best friend's wedding. When you walk into an arena or Shea Stadium and there are thousands of people there cheering, they already love you. They're there to drink in the godhead. At the wedding, every one of your human imperfections is there on display, and the worship of the godhead is not there to protect you. That small-level occasion is much more stressful than a huge concert."

WRAPPED AROUND YOUR FINGER

This song had a music video that was in constant rotation on MTV in 1983-84, exposing thousands of drummers to Stewart's playing and his octoban-accessorized kit. The song has an interesting approach to the groove, where for most of the song, there is only a backbeat on 4 (with 2 omitted). In the verses, this backbeat is a cross-stick, and the 1 is omitted on the bass drum. When coupled with Stewart's hi-hat artistry, this groove references the one-drop while putting it more in the realm of rock drumming. For the choruses, the backbeat on 4 moves to the open snare drum, and the 1 is played on the kick. While this groove isn't a baladi rhythm per se, the melody of the song and the choice of drum part does have hints of Arabic music.

Along with the basic groove construction, there are lots of interesting little embellishments all throughout the track. Stewart incorporates his splash cymbals, icebell, and motifs on the toms in various places. The fill leading back to the verse (measure 59) ascends the toms and ends on a splash, with the bass drum downbeat omitted. This approach appears in reggae and Arabic music, where embellishments end before the downbeat of the next bar, and Stewart's personal amalgamation of these styles uses this concept freely. Halfway through the fourth verse (measure 110), Stewart raises the energy and drive by shifting to a full 2-and-4 backbeat, which is maintained until the outro of the song. The incredibly crisp and clear recording and mixing of this track enable us to enjoy the depth of detail in the drumming.

"This was (a song) that in the take, I didn't really know what I was doing. I hadn't really grasped the rhythm of the track; I didn't really understand where the changes were; I didn't like the lyrics. I love all the songs, but this one would be at the bottom of my list—I just didn't get it. I enjoyed it live because I had my whole percussion rig with timpani and everything; it was glorious. You can go on YouTube and see the 'Stew cam' from the reunion tour, and it's just all my shit for the whole song. I had the timpani going, the xylophone, the crotales, and all this cool shit happening. The other guys had no idea what was going on behind them."

WRAPPED AROUND YOUR FINGER

Chorus 1

Interlude

Verse 3

WRAPPED AROUND YOUR FINGER

Chorus 3

Outro

WRAPPED AROUND YOUR FINGER

Fade Out

MURDER BY NUMBERS

"Murder by Numbers" is a triplet-based groove (written here in 12/8) that combines elements of several styles. The drums play an eight-bar intro in which Stewart creates a masterful "rhythmic illusion." The hi-hat plays all the eighths (in 12/8) while the bass drum essentially plays the backbeat. The thing that makes it tricky to the ear is the snare drum cross-stick, which plays every other eighth starting on the second one of the bar, essentially creating a quarter-note triplet feeling pushed back one eighth note. The way these things interlock can make certain listeners hear the one in the wrong place—or not know where it is at all. Bar 8 is the trickiest of all, where Stewart moves the bass drum to other notes in the bar. However, the intent is not to fool people; it grooves like crazy (once you have your bearings)!

The verses (starting in measure 17) use the same groove with tasty hi-hat accents and articulations improvised throughout, and the choruses (starting in measure 25) use a backbeat feel; this type of groove appears regularly in blues. Throughout the track, listen for Stewart's unique mastery of the hi-hat, adding accents of different dynamic and amount of opening of the cymbals, and the omission of bass drum notes in certain phrases of the verses. When the backbeat is introduced in the choruses, the drive increases, but is released when he goes back to the side stick in the second verse. Check out the interesting fill in measure 32: he plays a syncopated figure that ends on a splash, leaving out the 1 of the first bar of the verse. In the bridge (measure 81 to the end of the track), Stewart goes to the ride and creates a wonderful interplay of bell, bow, and crashed notes.

MURDER BY NUMBERS

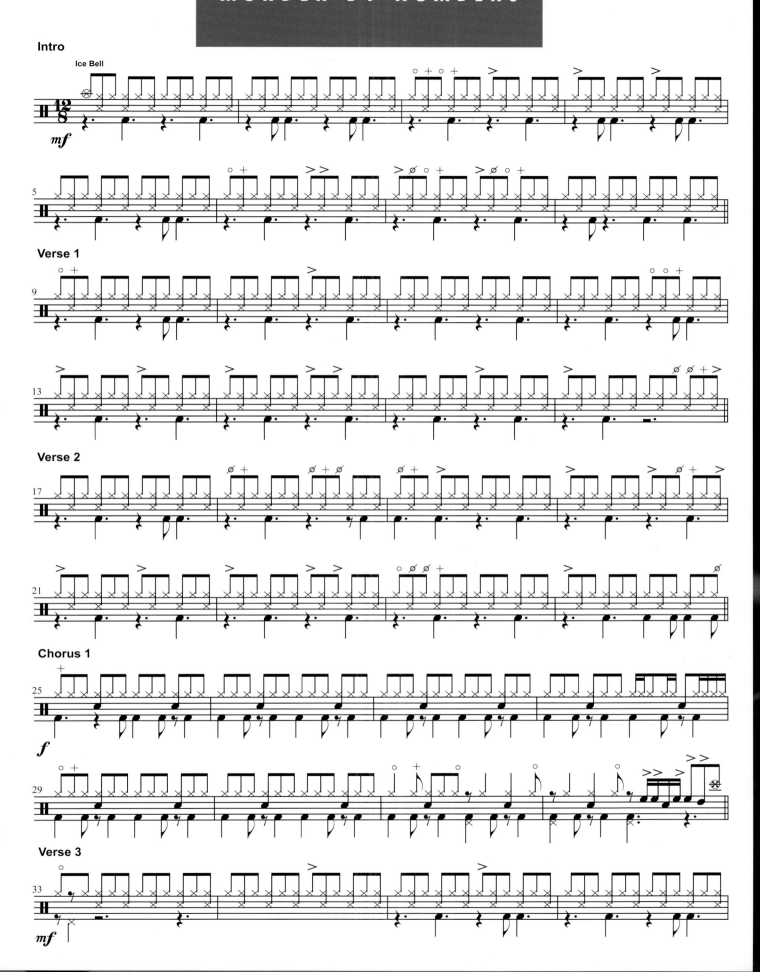

Intro

Verse 1

Verse 2

Chorus 1

Verse 3

MURDER BY NUMBERS

Chorus 3

December 18, 1979: Hammersmith Odeon, London. © Craig Betts

November 29, 1979: Palladium, New York (Photo by Dietmar Clös).

May 14, 1979: Dooleys, Tempe AZ (Photo by Lissa Wales).

Clockwise from top: July 23, 1983: *Synchronicity* tour, Comiskey Park, Chicago, Illinois (Photo by Paul Natkin). February 19, 1984: Rosemont Horizon, Rosemont, Illinois (Photo by Paul Natkin). 1983: *Synchronicity* tour (Photo by Danny Quatrochi).

SYNCHRONICITY II

(from *The Police Live!*) (Recorded 1983, released 1995)

In the recording studio, Stewart used effects, delays and overdubs, but these things don't change the fact that his is an entirely unique voice on the drums. When hearing The Police live, even if some of the overdubbed details were missing, you would still get the same vibe and excitement from Stewart's performance. "Synchronicity II," transcribed here from a performance that appears on *The Police Live!*, is a great example of this. On the album, there is a prominent overdub of a choked crash cymbal during the intro to the verses, which is missing in the live performance. Interestingly, Stewart does not try to play those accents with a choked hat, as would seem an obvious thing to do. The energy of the song is not affected.

This is a driving track, and Stewart plays it live with a relentless forward-pushing energy. There are differences between the album version and this live performance; as Stewart explained, in the studio many of the parts had just been made up, and they were different on other takes, so oftentimes these parts were not repeated. Stewart uses flams on the snare as a compositional tool to create an abrupt accent in the groove in various places. Verse 1 is a good place to hear this. Throughout the song there are also many foot hi-hat notes shown. Like many other drummers, Stewart's left foot was probably "dancing" on the hi-hat pedal as he grooved. We have notated the audible notes, but it's likely he was feeling a pulse of eighths with his foot in many of those places. This is an inspiring drum performance that is brimming with energy and fun to listen to.

This song appeared early in the set list on the *Synchronicity* tour. Did Stewart have a warm-up routine? "I hadn't yet discovered warming up yet. I think around that time I saw Tony Williams at a Stanley Clarke event, and he was warming up. I realized that I wished I could go on stage feeling as good playing the first song as I did playing the third song. It's really simple: Warm up! Since I hadn't yet discovered this back in The Police days, and I'd go out there cold. But I was young. I was into my roller skates at the time, and one of the cool things about arenas is that before they opened the doors, you could circle the whole thing on the marble floors. It was very relaxing. On a show day, you just want the hours to go by so that you can just walk on stage. Just killing time is something you try to do. Watching a movie doesn't really work. I found that meet-and-greets are a good way to eat up 45 minutes, and I do a lot of warming up now, because I can see the results. It's all about relaxing: you get more power when you're relaxed."

SYNCHRONICITY II

SYNCHRONICITY II

Pre-Chorus 1

Chorus 1

Verse 2

SYNCHRONICITY II

Pre-Chorus 2

Chorus 2

Instrumental

SYNCHRONICITY II

Edge of Ride

Vox In

Verse 3

SYNCHRONICITY II

Pre-Chorus 3

Top: August 2, 1983: The Spectrum Montreal. Bottom: January 21, 1980: Cleveland (Both photos courtesy of Dietmar Clös).

PART 3
SOLO WORKS

Backstage at Marquee Club, London, 1978 (© Craig Betts, Peter Baylis).

KLARK KENT
"TOO KOOL TO KALYPSO" (1979)

In 1977, The Police recorded a few songs with original guitarist Henry Padovani, mostly Stewart's compositions, but then Sting began writing heavily. Gigs had mostly dried up for The Police, and Stewart's other project, Klark Kent, began getting attention in the summer of 1978. He had a minor hit with "Don't Care" on his own Kryptone Records label, and when Klark Kent was booked to play on "Top of the Pops," Stewart felt that it would be lame to do it as a solo singer, so he brought his bandmates along to join him, all wearing masks.

It was the first time any of The Police had ever been on TV. While Klark Kent was experiencing success, Stewart was doing appearances and promo mainly by himself, and realized that it was lonely. A self-described "band guy," he was always happy to get back to his band mates, feeling better on "his team" rather than by himself. The Police were subsequently signed by A&M in the early summer.

"Too Kool to Kalypso" was recorded at Surrey Sound Studios on August 5, 1978. The verse groove for the song is layered together with multiple overdubs. While Stewart used some percussion instruments to create grooves, mostly he overdubbed different instruments from his drum set. A barely audible sixteenth-note pattern on either octobans, bongos, or roto-toms (the latter being more likely, since this was recorded before Stewart had octobans in his Tama kit) stretches under a simple drum set groove. On top of this, Stewart layered toms and cross sticks. There is also a cowbell part that continues through the verses. All of the layered parts give the section a "percussion ensemble of drum sets" effect.

The chorus is more bare-bones and has more of a punk aesthetic, with a driving double-time groove and bashy cymbals. The octoban/tom solo was simply a desire to "fill the bridge" with something different. Stewart recalls recording a few takes of drums for this section and then doing an edit with a cross-fade.

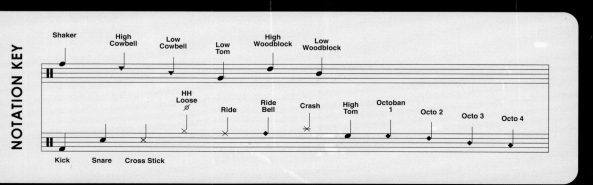

TOO KOOL TO KALYPSO

TOO KOOL TO KALYPSO

Chorus 1

TOO KOOL TO KALYPSO

TOO KOOL TO KALYPSO

Chorus 2

TOO KOOL TO KALYPSO

TOO KOOL TO KALYPSO

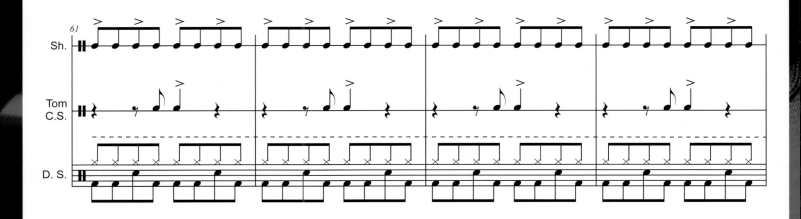

Verse 3

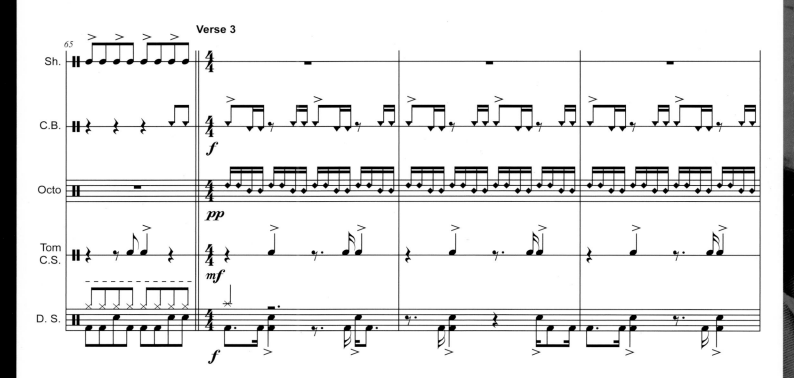

TOO KOOL TO KALYPSO

Chorus 3 / Outro

Begin Fade Out

TOO KOOL TO KALYPSO

Klark Kent, Covent Garden, London, July 23, 1978 (Photos © Craig Betts, Peter Baylis).

June 11, 1986: A Conspiracy of Hope Tour, Omni, Atlanta, GA (Photo courtesy Dietmar Clös).

RUMBLE FISH SOUNDTRACK (1983) "DON'T BOX ME IN"

In between *Ghost in the Machine* and *Synchronicity*, Stewart composed and recorded his first film soundtrack, for Francis Ford Coppola's *Rumble Fish*. Jeff Seitz recalls Stewart asking him to come out to California to work on it with him. "I was there in San Rafael for all the recording," says Jeff. "There were some recordings he did in a studio in Tulsa, where they had pile drivers, fans and clocks ticking. The famous typewriter drum solo was recorded there. They did more recording at Zoetrope, Coppola's studio in San Francisco." Originally Coppola though of using an additional composer and orchestrator, but after Stewart worked on the cues for a while, he secured sole possession of the composer's job for the film. Coppola dubbed the film at his house in Napa, where the director moved some of the cues to different places in the film. Jeff relates that Stewart was extremely positive in the face of multiple revisions, accommodating all the demands of the director with total professionalism, even when it meant another long night of composing new music.

"Don't Box Me In" reflects Stewart's creativity in constructing unique time feels in the studio. At first listen, the track sounds like a somewhat standard groove, but it has been creatively assembled with multiple tracks in the studio. There is a remnant of a drum machine part for just eight bars at the top (listen for obviously electronic kick and hi-hat), and then the rest of the song was created with a pile of bells in a hat playing sixteenths, and Stewart playing on two mic stands panned left and right in the mix in place of a hi-hat part. He then recorded a drum set part with acoustic bass drum and overdubs on toms and snare, mostly with brushes.

Stewart explained his approach to this track: "The only place you can hear the drum box (machine) is one of the snippets in the introduction before the track starts up," he said. "The first element to go down was the hat bells, which were a pile of finger cymbals in a hat. That's the eighth-note pattern. Then it was two tracks of sticks on mic stands for the eighth notes, kind of a clicky sound panned left and right, then drum set with brushes for the tom-toms and breaks. God knows how I kept the kick going so steady with my hands not working. The snare was always gated, sometimes for extreme effect. "

Note: This drum part shown on a grand staff, with the hat bells, sticks on mic stands, ride bell, and tambourine (all of which were overdubbed) shown on the top staff. The bottom staff shows the drum set, including the programmed parts.

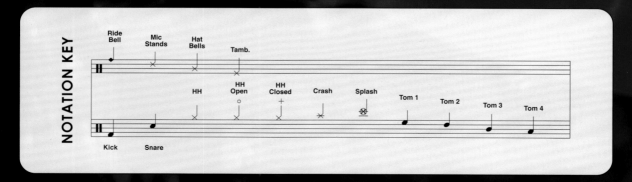

DON'T BOX ME IN

Intro

DON'T BOX ME IN

Verse 1

DON'T BOX ME IN

Chorus 1

Verse 2

DON'T BOX ME IN

Chorus 2

Overdubbed Snare On Beat 3 -

DON'T BOX ME IN

Harmonica Solo

Vocal

Chorus 3

Outro

Gradually crossfade hat bells and tamb.

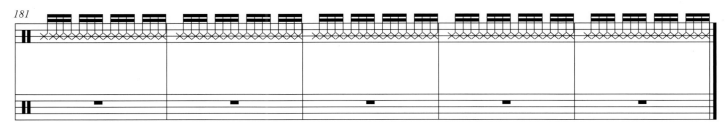

Fade out

In addition to a huge array of drums, Stewart's Sacred Grove studio is outfitted with an assortment of string, brass and percussion instruments (All photos courtesy Dietmar Clös).

THE RHYTHMATIST (1985)
"KOTEJA (OH BOLILLA)"

This song appears on *The Rhythmatist*, a 1985 release resulting from Stewart's journey to Africa to explore its rhythms and people. The record contains performances recorded in the field in Africa, as well as additional parts added in the studio.

After The Police disbanded, Jeff Seitz was working and performing around New Jersey when Stewart called again. "Stewart called and told me the engineer for his home studio had flaked out. For months I had been depositing my checks and waiting for something to happen (with The Police), but they were off doing their own thing. Stewart went to Africa and recorded *The Rhythmatist*. I had always thought about working in the studio, and I always had my hand in sound and running the P.A.; I was very into audio, so I went out to California and started working on *The Rhythmatist*. He showed me how to sync up tape machines and how to run his console, and our journey began. Then he got a feature called *Out of Bounds*, and then *The Equalizer* (TV series). Whenever we weren't working on *The Equalizer*, he would get another film."

There is a combination of electronic and acoustic sounds on this performance. Seitz co-produced and engineered *The Rhythmatist*, so he was able to shed some light on the construction of the drum part. The drum machine used was the Oberheim DMX, which was the second drum machine sold commercially after the Linn M-1. The basic structure of the drum part consists of kick and effected snare generated from the DMX, with Stewart playing acoustic drum set elements over it. The song starts this way and continues until verse 2 (bar 33), where Stewart adds cross-stick on the acoustic snare. The tom and octoban fills from this point to the end are all acoustic.

"There is also an eighth-note percussion rhythm that we used frequently called hat bells," says Seitz. "It was a cluster of finger cymbals laid loosely in the top of a cap, played with either mallets or sticks as an overdub. It can be confused with a hi-hat rhythm!"

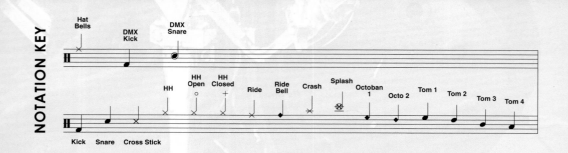

KOTEJA (OH BOLILLA)

KOTEJA (OH BOLILLA)

KOTEJA (OH BOLILLA)

KOTEJA (OH BOLILLA)

KOTEJA (OH BOLILLA)

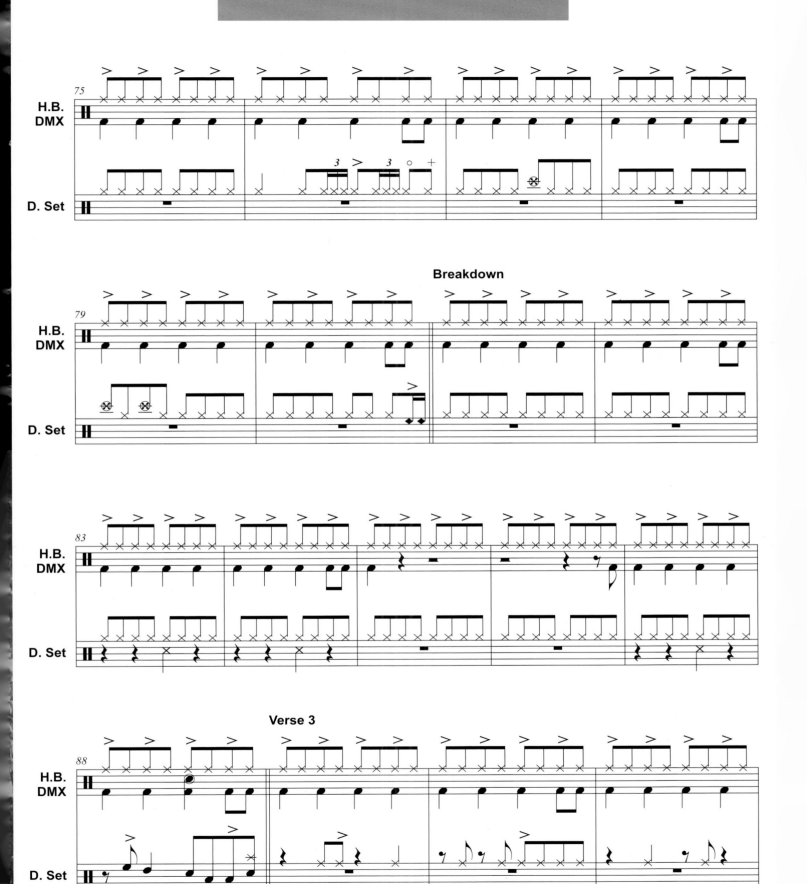

KOTEJA (OH BOLILLA)

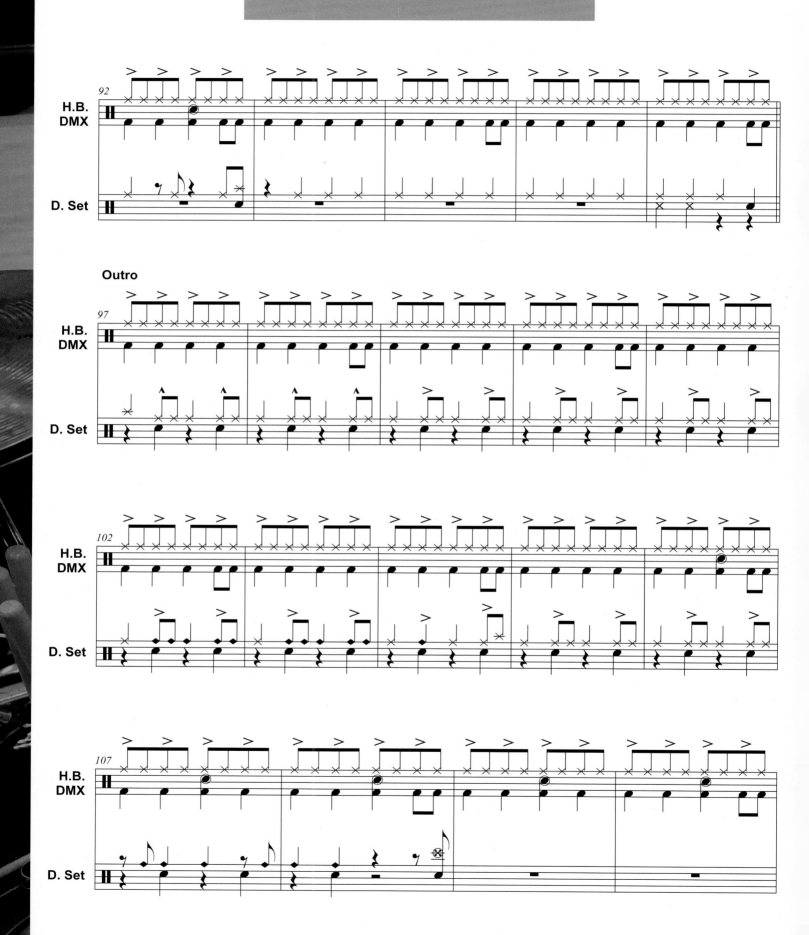

Outro

KOTEJA (OH BOLILLA)

KOTEJA (OH BOLILLA)

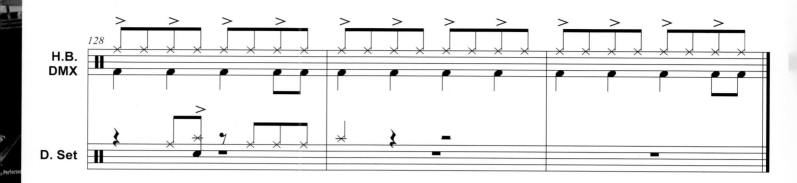

June 21, 2012, at Sacred Grove (Photo by Robert Downs).

PART 4
ANIMAL LOGIC
OYSTERHEAD &
GIZMODROME

At Sacred Grove (Photo courtesy Dietmar Clös).

ANIMAL LOGIC: *ANIMAL LOGIC* (1989)
"THERE'S A SPY (IN THE HOUSE OF LOVE)"

After The Police disbanded, Stewart formed the band Animal Logic with legendary bassist Stanley Clarke and songwriter/vocalist/guitarist Deborah Holland. They recorded two albums of melodic, memorable pop songs with creative, tight playing. "There's a Spy (In the House of Love)" is from their first album. Stewart creates unique grooves here, crafting a pattern for the verse that features his signature hi-hat work supporting a backbeat on the "and" of beat three. This gives the verse a wide feeling, and it creates release when he goes to the standard two-and-four on the snare in the choruses.

Stewart applies his signature technique of overdubbing sounds in the studio wherever he feels they will fit, but sparingly in this case. There is an interesting fill at measure 46 which sounds like a marching snare. This seems to be the only place in the song where an overdub or different sound was used, but it works perfectly in the track. Otherwise, the song is master class in tasteful application of technique and nuance to a pop drum part. Clarke's virtuosic bass playing and Stewart's unique drumming pair perfectly together with the song.

"With Animal Logic, our songwriter Deborah Holland did not have the status of having written hit albums, so Stanley and I could impose more wrong-headed musicality upon her songs than would have been possible if she had been a known songwriter," says Stewart. "We were able to take liberties that had only to do with musicality and little to do with serving the song. We took more of these liberties than we would in a normal pop group, and that affected how we arranged and recorded the music."

THERE'S A SPY
(IN THE HOUSE OF LOVE)

THERE'S A SPY
(IN THE HOUSE OF LOVE)

THERE'S A SPY
(IN THE HOUSE OF LOVE)

Chorus 3

Outro

Fade Out

OYSTERHEAD: *THE GRAND PECKING ORDER* (2001)
"RUBBERNECK LIONS"

Oysterhead was formed by bassist/vocalist Les Claypool of Primus and guitarist/vocalist Trey Anastasio of Phish, who recruited Stewart because he was one of their favorite drummers. The group recorded one album, *The Grand Pecking Order*, in 2001. In their jam band-type material, each of the three unique musicians can stretch out and add their musical personalities to the music.

"Rubberneck Lions" has a triplet feel, with Stewart shifting between quarter notes, a shuffled eighth feel, and quarter-note triplets on the bass drum. He shifts between the hi-hat and ride in various parts of the song, drawing various colors from the hats and ride, but in a much different context than The Police. Measures 72-83 contain some interesting drum breaks. The short bursts of single strokes on the snare and rollicking triplet fills are also quite a different flavor from The Police drum tracks.

The drum sound on this record is interesting; it captures Stewart's slappy snare and nuanced cymbals, but the tone is more aggressive than in The Police, and the toms are much deeper. Overall in his later recordings, his drum sound has trended this way.

"In Oysterhead, I don't think there was strategy or tactics," laughs Stewart. "We just jammed in the studio, and I cut up the jams. One of the other guys would get on the mic with lyrics, and we didn't do takes. We cut the music up after we had played things and made it into a track. Totally the wrong way to make a record!"

RUBBERNECK LIONS

RUBBERNECK LIONS

RUBBERNECK LIONS

RUBBERNECK LIONS

Chorus 2

Interlude

RUBBERNECK LIONS

RUBBERNECK LIONS

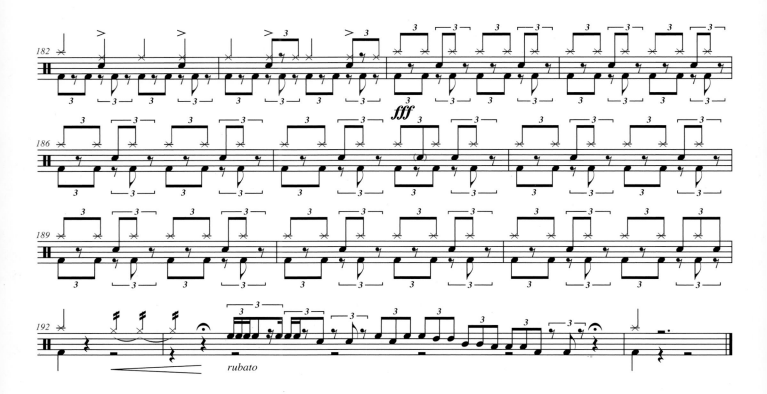

Top: With Oysterhead, 2000 (Photo by Paul Natkin). Bottom: Oysterhead rehearsal, Scranton, PA, July 2021 (Photo by Joe Bergamini).

GIZMODROME: *GIZMODROME* (2017)
"ZOMBIES IN THE MALL"

Gizmodrome is a progressive rock-style band featuring Stewart, Vittorio Cosma, Adrian Belew (King Crimson) and Mark King (Level 42). Their 2017 self-titled album features quirky material with Stewart stretching out into another sub-style of rock music. His signature style of drumming sounds at once familiar and yet different on this recording, and he also does most of the singing.

"Zombies in the Mall" is an interesting and challenging piece. We wrote it out here in 6/4 reflecting Stewart's phrasing, but the band plays essentially in three, giving the drum part a four-over-three feeling. Stewart varies the time feel by leaving out the snare drum in the first verse, then moving it around in different sections as the song progresses. Listen for some drum fills that sound straight out of jazz fusion. The intro groove (measure 4) contains a ghosted snare pattern that sounds very syncopated as it cycles over the "three" feel of the guitar and bass. Stewart changes the feel by dropping out the backbeats in the verses. He deconstructs the groove during the outro of the song, where he puts the backbeat on 3. The song has an unconventional form, with the verses treated differently and the two parts of the chorus not appearing in the same order.

The drum sound is compressed and saturated, making it difficult sometimes to tell the difference between a loose hi-hat and a bashy ride cymbal in the mix. The snare sound is different than other Stewart recordings; this one has a distinct "piccolo" sound, although it is his same Tama signature snare. It's an interesting example of how the same drum can sound totally different, depending on how it is played and recorded. Also listen for the occasional cymbal and gong drum overdub.

"Gizmo was a project where I'd go to Italy in the summer and make a deal with the mayor of a scenic village where they'd give us a church or somewhere to rehearse for two weeks in exchange for a show in the village square," says Stewart. "Me and some buddies would work up a set and go play shows across Italy. Every show was open air on a piazza somewhere. People didn't necessarily come to see me or Gizmo, it was just a beautiful evening and people would come out. It was summer and it was a fun thing to do. We were there for the pasta! That's what Gizmo was all about. Then one of my Italian buddies called and said there was a record company that wanted to put money into making an album. Armand (Sabal Lecco), couldn't (make it work), so I called Mark King. Vittorio had a line on Adrian Belew, so they both came out here. I cut those guys into the band, but I still got to dominate the record (laughs)." At this point the band name was changed to Gizmodrome, and this lineup recorded the album featuring "Zombies in the Mall."

ZOMBIES IN THE MALL

ZOMBIES IN THE MALL

ZOMBIES IN THE MALL

PART 5

GEAR &
TOUR SETUPS

Oysterhead rehearsal, July 2021 (Photo by Joe Bergamini).

Jeff Seitz has been Stewart's drum tech since January 20, 1980, joining him after the recording of *Reggatta de Blanc*. A Juilliard-educated musician, Jeff has pursued his own musical projects and remained active as a player during his entire association with Stewart. He continues to be Stewart's drum tech and production coordinator, assisting with all of his live projects. Jeff provided invaluable information for this section.

DRUMS

With The Police (in their original period, not the reunion tour), Stewart used three drum sets, all Tama. The first was a light blue Imperialstar that he acquired with his first Tama endorsement—an association that has lasted almost half a century. "In Curved Air I had a double-bass Ludwig Vistalite, my first record-company funded, professional kit," said Stewart. "I was reviewing gear for *Sounds* magazine, and I reviewed a set of Tama drums, and they blew everything else out of the water. It's hard to appreciate today how much Tama revolutionized drum gear. They really were a revolution in drum manufacturing, and the other companies had to catch up. The hardware made other brands look like toys. Also, the sound: the nine-ply drums with a painted interior just had a volume that was unmatched. It took a lot to give up my double bass monstrosity, but sound engineers were asking me to play the Tamas, because they sounded so good. I had to relearn how to get my groove on just one bass drum!"

Stewart used the original Tama kit on *Outlandos d'Amour* and *Reggatta de Blanc* and their subsequent tours, and then Tama gave him a new mahogany-finished Superstar kit that he used for recording *Zenyatta Mondatta*. Stewart didn't feel the Superstars responded as well in a live situation, so for *Ghost in the Machine* and *Synchronicity* he used a third kit, a dark blue Tama Imperialstar which was also used for the recording of those records.

Stewart's setup remained fairly constant with The Police, but there were some changes. The original powder blue Imperialstar kit had two rack toms, although there are photos from the early period where he had three mounted toms. He settled on the added 10" tom with the *Zenyatta* kit and kept all three racks through the end of the *Synchronicity* tour. For the reunion tour and his subsequent projects, he went back to two rack toms up front, sometimes placing the third tom to the left of his hi-hat, and changing from one floor tom to two.

Stewart began using Tama octobans as soon as they came

Stewart's setup March 23, 1982: *Ghost in the Machine* tour.
Courtesy of Jeff Seitz.

out. It's unclear when exactly he added them to his kit, but it was certainly sometime during the recording of *Reggatta de Blanc*. Tama sent Stewart a set of 8 octobans, which can be seen in photos of a gig at the London Lyceum on June 17, 1979, and in the "Message in a Bottle" video, but soon he settled on using four of them in his trademark "straight line" arrangement above his hi-hat. Stewart also made use of another Tama original instrument, the gong bass drum, but only as an overdub in the studio, never in his main kit. (The backbeats of "Every Breath You Take" were overdubbed with Stewart playing one hand on his snare and one on the gong drum, according to Seitz.) For live shows, the gong drum is incorporated into his percussion setup, separate from the kit.

The iconic snare drum that produced the classic sound that became Stewart's sonic fingerprint was a Pearl. Stewart isn't sure when he acquired the drum. "It is unknown when that drum came into my kit. Why would I have had a Pearl snare drum?" Jeff Seitz, after doing some research, has concluded it was acquired in the summer of 1979. There were actually two Pearl drums: one chrome over brass, and one chrome over steel. At first the drums were used interchangeably. It wasn't until the *Synchronicity* tour that the sound engineer picked the chrome-over-brass as "the one" with a brighter crack and larger decibel range. On the album recordings, Seitz believes both drums are heard on different tracks. Stewart cracked the original flanged batter hoops on the drums, so Jeff replaced them with die-cast Tama hoops.

Top: Pearl catalog photo showing snare drum model used by Stewart (Courtesy of Jeff Seitz).

Bottom: "The Snare": Stewart's Pearl snare, photographed at Sacred Grove by Dietmar Clös.

169

The snare drum batter head was tuned extremely tightly, with the bottom head tuned "normal tight," according to Seitz. The tom tom-heads were rarely changed, says Seitz. "For one thing, Stewart wasn't a big tom-tom player. And the heads sounded good. They were Remo Emperors, and they took the beating. I probably would have gotten more attack out of them if I had changed them more, but they sounded good."

On The Police reunion tour, Stewart used a brand new Tama Starclassic Maple kit with his Tama Signature Palette snare drum. The snare was matched by Tama's designers to sound like his original Pearl drum. Live recordings from that tour reveal the signature drum to sound nearly exactly like the original. Stewart reports it to feel the same as well, with the same snare response at all dynamic levels.

Stewart has also used all Tama hardware for many years. After seeing Slipknot in concert in 2000, he began using a double pedal. Interestingly, he places the slave pedal on the outside of the hi-hat pedal.

CYMBALS

Stewart began officially endorsing Paiste cymbals in March

1981 (according to the Paiste website), having begun playing them during the *Zenyatta Mondatta* tour. He can be seen using Zildjian cymbals in earlier photos. Stewart's cymbal setup was fairly consistent in terms of placement, although he has used different models of cymbals over the years. Known for his use of splash cymbals, he has had two of them in his setup starting with *Reggatta de Blanc*. Stewart's hi-hat work is the stuff of drum legend, and he favored Paiste 602 13" hi-hats once he signed with Paiste in 1981. His ride cymbal was a 24" Paiste RUDE Ride/Crash, and his crashes varied a little from tour to tour. In a 1982 *Modern Drummer* interview, Jeff Seitz cites the crashes as two 16" and two 18" RUDE Ride/Crashes, but Stewart would opt for thinner models in the studio (often 2002 or Formula 602 crashes). A Paiste 8" Bell and a UFIP Ictus 8" bell cymbal were also mainstays in his setup and appear prominently on several of the songs transcribed in this book.

A Paiste "Profiles" book of 1981, provided by Erik Paiste through Jeff Seitz, lists the following models as Stewart's setup:

- 13" Formula 602 Medium Hi-Hat

Left: Tama catalog image with Stewart Copeland Signature Snare (Courtesy of Tama Drums).
Right: Tama magazine ad featuring Tama Starclassic Maple kit made for The Police reunion tour (Courtesy Tama Drums).

- 8" 2002 Bell
- 14" RUDE Crash/Ride (or 16" 2002 Medium)
- 8" 2002 Splash
- 11" 2002 Splash
- 12" Formula 602 Paperthin Crash
- 16" Formula 602 Thin Crash
- 24" Formula 602 Heavy (or 22" RUDE Ride/ Crash)
- 16" RUDE Crash/Ride (or 18" 2002 Medium)

Although Stewart kept his cymbals loose on the stands, he did crack them often. Jeff Seitz reports that Stewart would crack the edges. "I've learned since then that the heavier the cymbal, the quicker it cracks," said Seitz. "We have thin and paper-thin crash cymbals for Stewart's orchestral work. He lays into them, but it's the same set we've been playing for over three years.

Stewart's current cymbal setup features his 22" Signature Series Blue Bell ride cymbal, 12" Signature Combo Crisp hi-hats, and Signature series crashes and splashes (lighter models than the RUDE series he played in the 1980s).

STICKS

Jeff Seitz believes that London Drum was where Stewart was getting his sticks when he first started as the drum tech. Regal Tip Rock Wood Tip model is what he used from approximately 1981 to 1999, then he signed with Vater, who currently manufactures his signature stick, the Stewart Copeland Standard. He also uses Mike Balter Lexan #92F mallets.

ELECTRONICS AND OTHER GEAR

Stewart experimented with and used delay effects on his drums starting right after the recording of *Outlandos d'Amour*. These effects can be heard very clearly on "Walking on the Moon" and "Reggatta de Blanc," as well as "One World," "Every Little Thing She Does is Magic" and other tracks. This, along with overdubbing parts in the studio, makes his recorded work challenging to decipher and transcribe. Some of the patterns resulting from the delay are essentially unplayable by a single human drummer without the effects. Stewart utilized the delay effects live as well, and they became a part of his performance vocabulary such that he would play off the delayed-produced notes and improvise with them.

Regarding the effects and delays used live, Jeff Seitz recalls that different parts of the kit would be input

Top: Paiste ad circa 1983. Bottom: Paiste Stewart Signature Ride ad.

to the delay unit, depending on which song was being performed. "There were delay settings for each song, in milliseconds," said Seitz. "Sometimes it would be just snare, or hi-hat and snare, but often octobans, because he wanted them to repeat. So, it was a pre-set arrangement with the monitor engineer; he had a chart, and he knew which drums would be sent to the delay on which songs. Prior to that, Stewart and I would do it verbally with the monitor engineer, but starting with the *Ghost* tour, the monitor engineer had a pre-set for each song, and I would change the delay settings manually (because this was before MIDI and program changes, etc.). On the reunion tour, we used newer technology. In the studio, the delay was always created at the board using studio units (not by Stewart's gear), but with Stewart's instructions.

"Stewart started using the delay as an outcropping of dub and reggae," continues Seitz. "He got himself an extra microphone, put it in the bass drum, and plugged it into a Fender Twin. Before I got the gig he was using a Roland Chorus Echo (301), and he would create his own delay stuff out of a Roland JC 60 or Fender Twin speaker cabinet, and have the soundman mic it up. When I got the gig, they were already taking a D.I. out of the echo unit, running it to the monitor board and feeding it back

Roland Chorus Echo at Sacred Grove. Photo by Dietmar Clös.

through the monitors.

"The only trigger pickup we had on the drums when I started with Stewart was on the kick drum, which was fed into a Tama Snyper DS200 drum synthesizer. It was for producing low end effects. Stewart had a foot pedal, and he would switch it on and off. There was also a time when he had a Remo roto-tom with a pickup that was fed into the DS200 (which had two mono channels), to give a pitch-bended tom effect when he hit it.

In certain photos of the *Ghost in the Machine* era, other instruments are visible in Stewart's setup. For a time he had two additional rack toms to his left, both fed into a second DS200 for effect. The DS200 could accommodate two pitches, so one of the left-side toms was set up to play "Invisible Sun," with its low-pitched "Syndrum" sound, and the other a higher-pitched effect. On the *Ghost* tour, Stewart also had a set of temple blocks, which he would use whenever the inspiration arose (often on "Spirits in the Material World," according to Seitz), and a cowbell. On the *Synchronicity* tour there were two cowbells, one on each side of the octobans. He tried Simmons drums as well at the start of the *Synchronicity* tour but he hated how they felt, according to Seitz, so he opted for the acoustic toms with triggers attached.

The photo below shows the delay and the Tama Snyper DS200 rack (not fully in view) with setlist and delay settings. From the top:

1. Two D.I. boxes
2. DS200
3. DS200
4. DeltaLab DL-4 Time Delay Digital Delay Performer Series
5. DeltaLab Memory Module (extra delay length)
6. AMS DMX 15-80 Digital Delay (later replaced with another DeltaLab DL-4 as backup)

On The Police reunion tour (2007-2008), Stewart continued using electronic effects, and the technology of

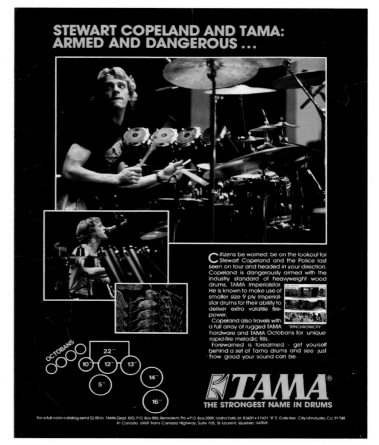

1983 Tama ad.

them had, of course, evolved considerably by that time. There was a trigger on the snare drum for "Invisible Sun." and a MalletKAT on the percussion riser which was used for "Walking in Your Footsteps." On this tour, Jeff Seitz had all the drums coming into a mixer at his station, where he had presets for the drums that would be sent into the delay for each song.

View of kit showing rack-mounted gear, *Ghost in the Machine* tour (Photo by Jeff Seitz). Left: Stewart performance at PASIC 1985, Jeff Seitz at right. Note Tama drum synthesizers in rack (Photo by Lissa Wales).

Instruments at Stewart's Sacred Grove studio (all photos courtesy Dietmar Clös).

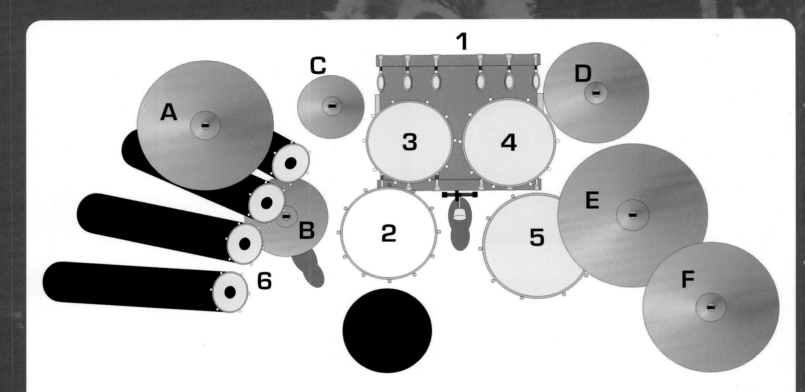

DRUMS

Tama Imperialstar, light blue finish

1. 14x22 bass drum

2. 5x14 Tama King Beat metal snare
   (Pearl snare B4514 chrome over brass
   was acquired sometime after the
   recording of *Regatta de Blanc*.)

3. 8x12 tom

4. 9x13 tom

5. 16x16 floor tom

6. Octobans – low-pitched set of 4

CYMBALS

(pre-endorsement) Zildjian

A. 16" Crash

B. 14" Hi-Hats

C. 10" Splash

D. 16" Crash

E. 22" Ride

F. 18" Crash

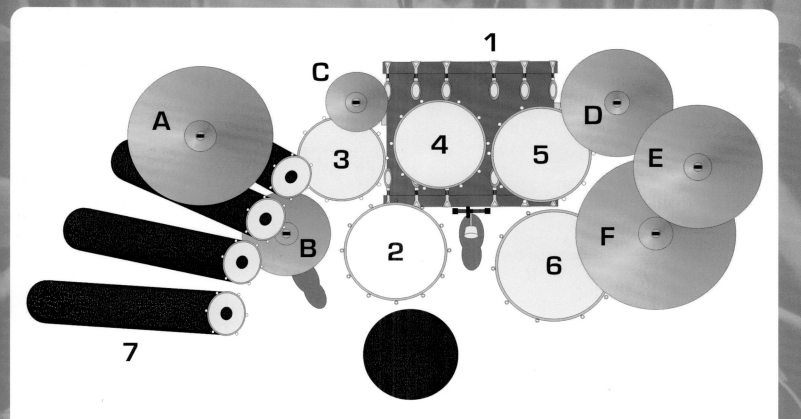

DRUMS

Tama Superstar, mahogany finish

1. 14x22 bass drum
2. 5x14 Pearl snare (B4514 chrome over brass)
3. 8x10 tom
4. 8x12 tom
5. 9x13 tom
6. 16x16 floor tom
7. Octobans – low-pitched set of 4

CYMBALS

Zildjian (for recording of album)

A. 18" Thin Crash
B. 14" New Beat Hi-Hats
C. 8" Splash
D. 16" Thin Crash
E. 18" Thin Crash
F. 22" Ping Ride

NOTES

The Tama Superstar kit used for the recording of *Zenyatta Mondatta* was soon retired, as Tama sent a new Imperialstar kit that Stewart preferred. By the time of the *Zenyatta* tour, the Pearl snare had made its way into Stewart's setup, and the cymbal setup was expanded. It was at this time that Stewart began to check out Paiste cymbals, soon to become an endorser. The bass drum and a Remo roto-tom were fitted with triggers that fed a Tama Snyper DS-200 drum synthesizer for live shows. This kit is now owned by Jeff Seitz.

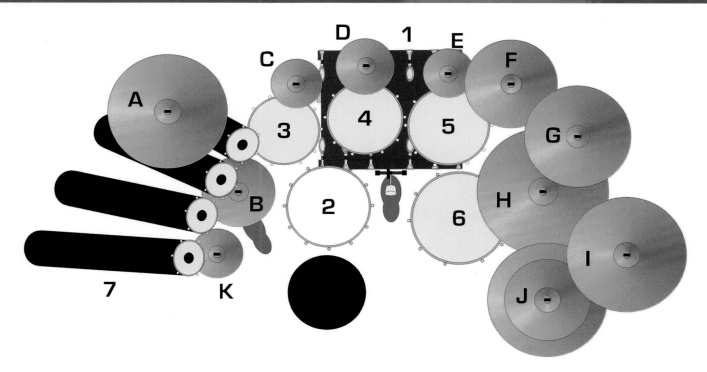

DRUMS

Tama Imperialstar, midnight blue finish

1. 14x22 bass drum

2. 5x14 Pearl snare (B4514 chrome over brass)

3. 8x10 tom

4. 8x12 tom

5. 9x13 tom

6. 16x16 floor tom

7. Octobans – low-pitched set of 4

CYMBALS

Paiste (except as noted)

A. 18" 2002 Crash

B. 13" Formula 602 Hi-Hats

C. 8" UFIP Ictus bell cymbal

D. 10" 2002 Splash

E. 8" 2002 Splash

F. 16" RUDE Ride/Crash

G. 16" RUDE Ride/Crash

H. 24" RUDE Ride

I. 18" 2002 Crash

J. 22" 2002 China Type

K. 8" 2002 Bell

ELECTRONICS

Effects rack to left of hi-hat:

1. Tama DS200

2. Simmons SDSV Analog Drum Brain

3. Tama DS200

4. DeltaLab Memory Module (extra delay length)

5. DeltaLab DL-4 Time Delay Digital Delay Performer Series

6. DeltaLab DL-4 Time Delay Digital Delay Performer Series (spare backup)

HEADS

Remo Ambassador on snare, coated Emperors on tom batters, coated Ambassadors on tom resonants, Black Dot on bass drum and octobans.

The same drum set was used on *Ghost in the Machine* and both the *Ghost* and *Synchronicity* tours. On the *Ghost* tour, some of the cymbal selections may have been different, and there were two additional Tama toms (8x12 and 9x13) to Stewart's left (which were used to trigger effects), a set of Ludwig temple blocks, and a cowbell. None of these were used in the studio as part of the main setup. On the *Synchronicity* tour, Stewart also used 2 LP cowbells, 2 Simmons pads (later changed to the 8x12 and 9x13 toms), and 3 Tama Snyper Triggers (1 on the kick drum for low end, 1 each on the toms).

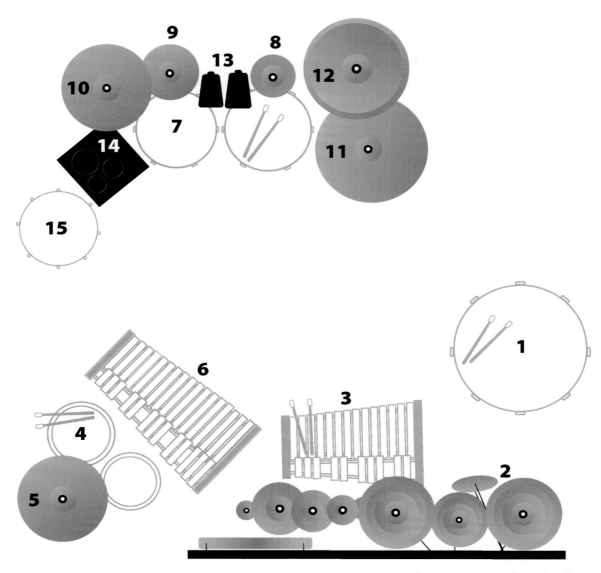

Diagram courtesy of Joe Gorelick

PERCUSSION RISER

The *Synchronicity* tour percussion riser consisted of the following:

1. Tama gong drum (riser downstage stage right)

2. Paiste - assorted cymbal and gong percussion rack (riser rear left)

3. Musser xylophone (riser rear in front of Paiste rack)

4. Latin Percussion congas (riser left corner rear)

5. Paiste 602 16" Crash cymbal (riser left corner rear in behind the congas)

6. Bergerault Glockenspiel Radio France - 3 oct. F5 to E8 (riser left corner rear in front of the congas)

7. Latin percussion timbales (riser front stage)

8. Paiste 2002 8" Splash cymbal (riser front behind the timbales)

9. Paiste 2002 10" Splash cymbal (riser front behind

the timbales)

10. Paiste 2002 12" Flanger cymbal (riser front behind the timbales)

11. Paiste 2002 18" Crash cymbal stacked (riser front behind the timbales)

12. Paiste 2002 20" China cymbal stacked (riser front behind the timbales)

13. Latin Percussion cowbells (riser front behind the timbales)

14. Electronic drum pad (brand unknown) (riser front to the left of electronic drum pad)

15. Tama Imperialstar 5x14 Snare drum

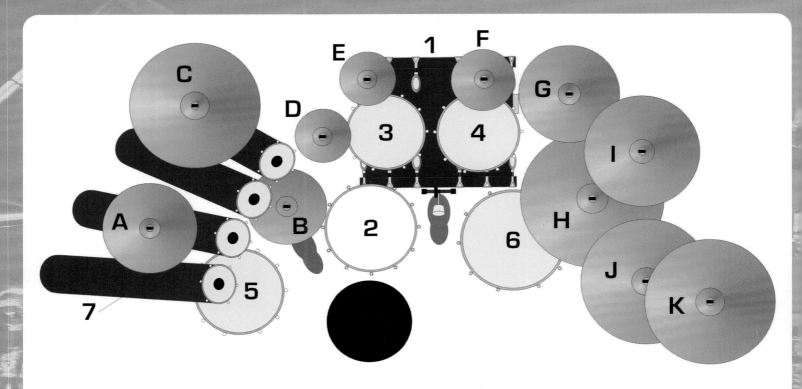

DRUMS

Tama Starclassic Maple, "Police blue" sparkle finish

1. 18x22 bass drum

2. 5x14 Stewart Copeland Signature Palette snare drum

3. 8x10 tom

4. 9x13 tom

5. 8x12 tom

6. 16x16 floor tom

7. 16x18 floor tom

8. Octobans – low-pitched set of 4

CYMBALS

Paiste

A. 14" 2002 Flanger Splash

B. 12" Signature Combo Crisp Hi-Hats

C. 18" Signature Fast Crash

D. 8" Signature Bell

E. 8" Signature Splash

F. 10" Signature Splash

G. 16" Signature Full Crash

H. 22" Signature Blue Bell Ride

I. 17" Signature Fast Crash

J. 18" Traditionals Light Flat Ride

K. 18" Signature Fast Crash

HEADS

Remo coated Emperor on snare, clear Emperor tom batters, Remo clear Ambassador on tom resonants, Powerstroke 3 bass drum batter, Black Dot on octobans.

Stewart also used a percussion rig containing Adams 26" and 32" timpani, Tama 8" and 10" Mini-Tymps, a Paiste 18" Wild Crash, 16"x20" Tama gong bass drum, a cymbal rack custom modified by Tait Towers, Paiste 2½ octave crotales, a MalletKAT 5 sending MIDI to a Kurzweil K2500RS sampler, and a Paiste 60" gong.

The Tama Stewart Copeland Artist Palette Signature Snare Drum was modeled by Tama after Stewart's classic Pearl drum, with similar brass shell composition, and a hoop configuration consisting of a die-cast hoop on the batter side and a flanged hoop on the resonant side. Listening to recordings and videos from the reunion tour, it sounds almost exactly like his old drum.

Stewart and Jeff graciously invited me to a rehearsal for Oysterhead's 2021 performance at Scranton's Peach Music Festival. I was able to get an up-close look at Stewart's kit. His gear is truly a reflection of his unique personality as a drummer.

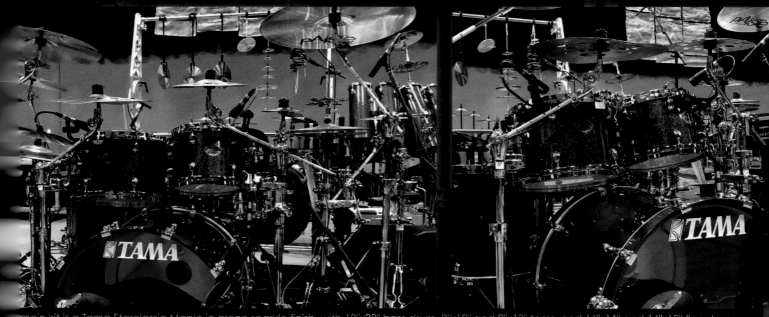

main kit is a Tama Starclassic Maple in green sparkle finish, with 18"x22" bass drum, 8"x10" and 9"x13" toms, and 16"x16" and 16"x18" floor toms.

art employs a large percussion setup at the rear of the stage mounted on the rack that was custom-built for The Police reunion tour by Tait Towers. ded are a mounted djembe, 20" gong bass drum, 4 octobans, a 12x26" bass drum, crotales, and various cup chimes, splashes, and small cymbals. setup is played standing up. All photos by Joe Bergamini.

In addition, Stewart also had the following on the Oysterhead kit: a Latin Percussion 6" Micro Snare mounted to the left of the hi-hat (between the hi-hat and 8" Signature Bell), and a Latin Percussion City Series Hi-Hat Jingle Ring Double attached to the hi-hat rod.

Stewart's signature Tama snare drum.

Stewart places his left-foot slave bass drum pedal on the outside of his hi-hat pedal, in order to keep the hi-hat closer. He sometimes will play the left kick pedal with his heel.

A simple foot switch allows Stewart to turn the delay on and off, while Jeff switches patches from his station at stage left. There's also an alarm pedal attached by velcro to Stewart's drinks table that he can push if there is a problem with the drums or himself.

The button activates a red light located on the delay switching module at Jeff's station. The module and pedals were custom built by UK electronics wizard Pete Cornish.

Stewart's longtime tech, Jeff Seitz, keeps everything tweaked to perfection.

A green version of Stewart's signature Paiste 22" Rhythmatist ride was made for the Oysterhead

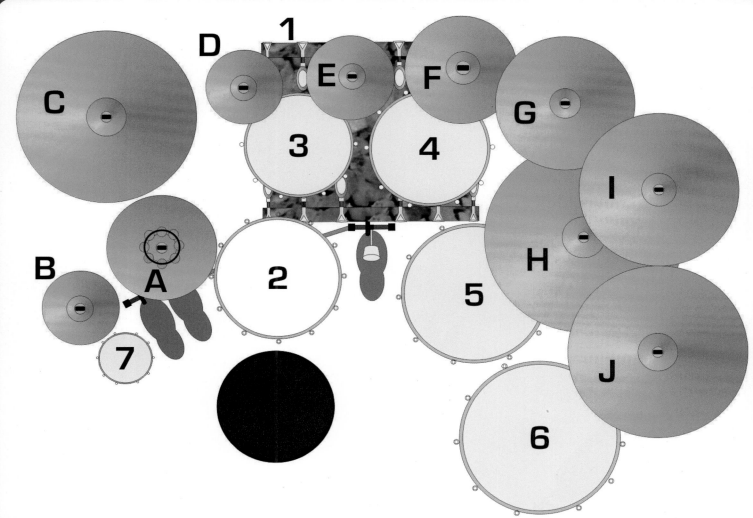

DRUMS

Tama Starclassic Maple (various finishes)

1. 18x22 bass drum

2. 5x14 Stewart Copeland Signature Palette snare drum

3. 8x10 tom

4. 9x13 tom

5. 16x16 floor tom

6. 16x18 floor tom

7. LP 6" Micro-Snare

CYMBALS

Paiste

A. 12" Signature Combo Crisp Hi-Hats (with LP City Series Hi-Hat Jingle Ring Double mounted on hi-hat rod)

B. 8" Signature Bell

C. 18" Formula 602 Classic Paper Thin Crash

D. 6" Signature Splash

E. 10" PSTX Swiss Splash

F. 14" PSTX Swiss Flanger Crash

G. 16" Formula 602 Classic Thin Crash

H. 22" Twenty Custom Full Ride

I. 18" Formula 602 Classic Thin Crash

J. 20" Formula 602 Classic Medium Flat Ride

ABOUT THE AUTHOR

Joe Bergamini's extensive Broadway resume includes holding the drum chair for *Gettin' the Band Back Together* (2018) and performing over 15 other Broadway shows as a sub, including *Beautiful (The Carole King Musical); Movin' Out; Jersey Boys; Pippin; Jesus Christ Superstar; Million Dollar Quartet; Rock of Ages; In the Heights, The Lion King*, and others. A member of prog rock bands Happy the Man and 4Front, he appeared on the first national tour of *Movin' Out* and currently tours internationally with The Doo-Wop Project.

Joe has run his own private teaching studio for over 30 years and has been the director of the Sabian Education Network since 2015. As Senior Drum Editor for Hudson Music since 2009, he has worked with Neil Peart, Steve Gadd, Steve Smith, David Garibaldi, Mark Guiliana and many others on their educational products. An active clinician, he has given hundreds of drum clinics in schools, universities, and at drum festivals worldwide.

The author of 12 drum books, Joe has won four *Modern Drummer* Readers Poll awards. He proudly endorses Tama drums, Sabian cymbals, Vic Firth sticks, Evans drumheads, and Latin Percussion.

For more about Joe, please visit:

joebergamini.com

facebook.com/joebergaminidrums

instagram.com/joebergamini

youtube.com/user/joebergaminidotcom

ALSO BY JOE BERGAMINI

Neil Peart: Taking Center Stage

The Working Drummer's Chart Book

Arrival Drum Play-Along

MD Classic Tracks: The World's Greatest Drummers Note for Note

Drum Techniques of Led Zeppelin

Operation Rockenfield: The Drumming of Queensryche

Pedal Control (with Dom Famularo)

It's Your Move (with Dom Famularo)

ACKNOWLEDGMENTS & SOURCES

Stewart Copeland for his time in new interviews and much assistance in connecting us with other contributors.

Jeff Seitz for new interviews and assistance with gear research, recording analysis, fact-checking and editing the "gear" section, and other information.

Dietmar Clös, co-founder of The PoliceWiki, for photos, ads, chronology, and additional editing.

Jim Gallagher at Hoshino (U.S.A.)/Tama Drums for ads and photos.

Craig Betts for access to many great, rare photos.

TRANSCRIPTIONS

"Roxanne," "Can't Stand Losing You," "Driven to Tears," "Spirits in the Material World," and "Every Little Thing She Does is Magic" transcribed by Joe Bergamini.

"One World (Not Three)," "Too Kool to Kalypso," "Don't Box Me In," "Koteja (Oh Bolilla)," "There's a Spy (In the House of Love)," "Rubberneck Lions," and "Zombies in the Mall" transcribed by Christian Johnson.

"Message in a Bottle," "Walking on the Moon," "Don't Stand So Close to Me," "Wrapped Around Your Finger," and "Synchronicity II (Live)" transcribed by Mike Sorrentino.

"Murder by Numbers" transcribed by Brad Schlueter.

SOURCES

Author interviews with Stewart Copeland

Author interviews with Jeff Seitz

Author correspondence with Dietmar Clös, The PoliceWiki

Modern Drummer magazine: October 1982, April 1990, June 2018 interviews

The Police Live! DVD (1995)

Everyone Stares: The Police Inside Out DVD

Strange Things Happen by Stewart Copeland

The Sessions online interview with Dom Famularo (Online interview)